AMAZING WHITETAILS

AMAZING WHITETAILS

Photography and Text
By
Mike Biggs

Published by
T. P. W., Inc.
Fort Worth, Texas

AMAZING WHITETAILS.

Copyright © 1994 Mike Biggs

Published by:
T. P. W., Inc.
P.O.Box 330787
Fort Worth, Texas 76163

Printed in the United States of America
Second Edition

Edited by Aaron Fraser Pass

Layout and design by Mike Biggs.

Library of Congress Catalog Card Number: 94-61042

ISBN 0-9642915-0-9

DEDICATION

A SPECIAL EDITION FOR
NORTH AMERICAN HUNTING CLUB MEMBERS

At the North American Hunting Club we judge everything we do by two criteria. First is "Will this help NAHC members enhance their hunting skills and enjoyment?" The second is, "Is this the best service or product we can possibly provide to members?"

When we took a look at the book you have in your hands, our answer to both questions was a loud, unison "Yes!" This is the best whitetail book of its kind we've ever seen. Of course, working with photographer/writer Mike Biggs, we should have figured it would be. Mike has been providing some of the best covers and feature photography for North American Hunter magazine for many years.

I don't think there's anyone who will put this book down without learning something new or seeing something they've never seen a whitetail do before. It's that good!

Best Afield,

Bill Miller
Executive Director
North American Hunting Club

Dedication

To my mother, Tommye Ruth Baxter, who has always been there with encouragement and support. When I was growing up, she picked me up, dusted me off, and put me back on the right track more times than I can remember. If she had a nickel for every time she ever drove me to a distant farm pond, arrowhead field, camp-out or other adventure, or for all the times she suffered through my countless outdoor "war stories," she'd be a rich woman.

To "Granny" Baxter, whose tall tales of camping and hunting and fishing "when she was a little boy" at the turn of the century, made us all wish we could have been there. This book would be much more colorful and interesting had she written it. Perhaps in some ways, she did.

..... Mike Biggs

CONTENTS

Acknowledgements

Outstanding personal accomplishments are rarely the result of one man's efforts alone. While it's true that the one man may have gone through a lot ...it's also true that through the help of others, the quality of the resulting achievement is magnified many times over. I would never have reached the point where this book would even be possible, without the help of many, many people. I am sincerely thankful to this large and very diverse group of friends and acquaintances who have helped me so much along the way. I thank you all.

Here, I'd like to make special mention of a few of the people who have helped me toward this project in one way or another ...in no particular order whatsoever.

David Morris ...a fine and most talented southern gentleman from Montana.

George & Elizabeth Jambers ...kind, wonderful people, and fine stewards of the land.

Mr. & Mrs. C.W.Cain ...who opened their doors and made me feel like family.

All **the Avants, Joan, J.R., Jeff,** and **Tracy** ... I could never have done it without you.

Bud Richter ...I never knew Californians could be so nice. You're a true friend.

David Lee ...who else could I call from a remote cabin in the middle of a raging flood, at 4:00 A.M. in the morning?

Buddy & Tommie Lowery ...so many irons in the fire, yet always willing to help.

Dave Fulson ...Elmer Fudd reincarnated. A great helper when I really needed one.

Tom Mantzel ...who gave me my first key to a ranch, when nobody had ever heard of me.

All **the Schreiners,** especially **Louie** ...who always made sure I was well taken care of.

Gordon Whittington ...at the top of his trade. Thanks for helping along the way.

Joe & Karen Langdon ...great friends, who live where the deer and the buffalo roam.

Kermit Klaerner ...whose kindness to strangers has made his deer famous.

Dr. James Kroll ...the best in the business. "Dr. Deer" knows about whitetails.

Gene Riser, and the whole Riser family ...working hard to raise those deer.

Cricket Heumann ...a finer friend or hunting partner would be hard to come by.

David & Beverly Cummings ...great people, who have an incredibly beautiful place.

Wyman Meinzer ...whose compelling photographic talents inspired me.

Billy Powell & Cliff Powell ...who always leave the door open, and hold a place at the table. Thanks. It means a lot.

Thompson Temple ...who went out of his way to help, way back in the beginning.

Dr. Harry Jacobson ...a great researcher, whose help has been invaluable.

Jerry Smith & John Wooters ...a great photographer and a great writer, whose earlier book helped set the stage.

Bill Carter ...a whitetail manager unlike any other. Thanks for your help.

Charlie Alsheimer ...a good friend, a top-notch photographer, and a whitetail "nut".

Mark Ellett & Bob Ellett ...who run a great operation, with incredible hospitality.

Larry Grimland & Allen Grimland ...doing a great job with their deer.

Lew Thompson & all the owners ...one of the best run operations in the world.

Thanks to **Judy Ashworth, Wes Wynne, Cecil Carder, Craig Boddington, Jack Brittingham, Glenn Sodd, A.C. Parsons, Cheryl Davenport, Jimmy Jones, Bob Cook, Bruce Williams, Kelly Snodgrass, Grady Allen, Jerry Daniels, Gerald Ryals, Don Keller, Gene Fuchs, Ray Sasser, Nick Gilmore, Mike Love, Gary Martin, Jack Cooper, Johnny Johnson, Dan Cox, Joel Benavides, Tom Evans, Richard McCarty, Harold Jambers, Jr., Rusty Dawkins, Bill Morrill, Judd Cooney, Donnie Schuch, Aaron Pass**, and many others.

Thanks to my son, **Brad**, and thanks to my very best friend, **Angela Casteel**, for sticking with me through thick and thin.

Foreword

by
Dr. James C. Kroll

It has been my pleasure to work intimately with whitetails for more than twenty-five years. When I first began working with the species, interest centered primarily on hunting. More recently, however, I have seen a dramatic shift in perspective, both by the hunting and non-hunting public. A new generation is assuming leadership, and there is a broad transition in progress. Whitetail hunters and enthusiasts alike are becoming *whitetail managers*, as well. Whereas our fathers hunted whitetails just for meat and sport, the modern deer hunter wants to give something back to the species. He wants to know more about the intimate lives of these amazing animals; not just to become a better hunter, but because he truly cares about whitetails. Non-hunters as well are more interested in deer. In many regions, deer have become increasingly numerous. This has created an expanded awareness, and has generated a great deal of interest in learning more about whitetail behavior and biology. These animals lead fascinating lives, and it seems that the more people know about them, the more they want to know.

Over the years I have observed many unusual whitetail behaviors, each time wishing — if only I had a photograph. Then one day I opened a magazine and there, in vivid color, was one of these unique behaviors! My eye moved quickly to the by-line: **Mike Biggs.** "Now this is a refreshing change," I mused. And it was. I had seen too many simple deer portraits and too few interesting or biologically significant images of whitetails as they really are.

Then came a rapid succession of ever-amazing images, each revealing some new marvel about the intimate life of the whitetail. I decided this was a man I needed to meet. I not only met Mike, but he has become a valued friend and colleague. We have hunted and studied deer together, and shared our love for deer.

It is rare when a man becomes an icon; especially in these days of fallen heroes. But Mike Biggs **is** an icon. Among whitetail enthusiasts, his name has become synonymous with quality deer photography. He is real; a man of integrity and dedication. Through his incredible images he has given us insight into the daily lives of deer, more than any other outdoor photographer. And now, he has compiled his greatest works into a single book.

Amazing Whitetails clearly will become the standard in deer books. There is nothing else like it. It deals with more detail than any book ever published on deer. It does what every deer book should do; it entertains, as well as teaches. If you read and study this book, you **will** know a great deal more about whitetails.

..........................J.C.K.

Introduction

There were a lot of advantages to growing up in a small town. I didn't exactly live on a farm or ranch, but probably half of my friends and acquaintances did. That being the case, I spent most of my formative years growing up in frequent contact with rural and outdoor environments. Early on, I was introduced to dairy cows, goats, horses, and other farm animals. I made friends with sheep dogs and bird dogs, and time spent in farm country nurtured an early interest in the outdoors in general. I eagerly traversed a wide spectrum of interests common to young naturalists everywhere. As a kid I was an enthusiastic rockhound, a budding entomologist, an amateur archaeologist, a studious mammologist and a piscatorial predator who knew no bounds. I lived for the sights, sounds, smells and solitude of the outdoors. I spent hundreds, perhaps thousands, of hours investigating the wonders of farm ponds and backwoods pastures, on my own. I was absolutely fascinated by "boss" bullfrogs, any largemouth bass over two pounds, jackrabbits and especially by the Indian arrowheads that I found during my explorations. The idea that there had been mysterious, unknown hunters in these private places long before me was intriguing to say the least.

By the time I was about 10 or 11 years old, my dance card was pretty full, where hunting and fishing and the outdoors were concerned. In between the obligatory time spent in classrooms, time spent with fami-

ly and short breaks for eating and sleeping, were as many outdoor adventures as I could wrangle my way into. Of course, we're not exactly talking world-wide excursions here, but it didn't matter to me. The Wolfe family had a great five-acre lake at the edge of town where I had permission to fish. The Boyd farm, six miles south, was a terrific place to hike the countryside looking for arrowheads and adventure. I could always take my dog and go tromping through the brush and the pecan orchards behind the Cason's house, or there was the two-acre pond surrounded by willows across the field from my home. It was filled with bass, and frogs, and snakes, and all the fishing lures I'd snagged in the willows. All things considered, I figured I was a pretty lucky kid.

I had dreamed of hunting and fishing in exotic places, where the fish were all 10 pounders, where the hills were filled with deer and mountain lions and where unthinkable adventures were commonplace. But, these things and places were simply beyond my grasp. While I had been well introduced to fishing and small game hunting, no one in our family had much experience with larger game.

Then, a remarkable thing happened. Through a chain of unlikely circumstances and events, I was invited by some acquaintances of the family to go on a whitetail hunt. I went through months of great anticipation, spellbound by the stories of deer, wild turkey and other wildlife which supposedly abounded at our destination.

It was my first trip into truly remote, utterly wild country, and I was mesmerized by the scope of the adventure. The six-hour drive to get there seemed endless. It was an old-time deer camp which consisted primarily of an ancient gray wood shack which might have measured fifteen feet square at the most. By all appearances, it had been there since the beginning of time. There was also a large tent and a fireplace outside. About three hundred yards down the hill there was a rock-filled creek flowing with cold, clear water. It was lined with red oaks and hackberrys in fall color, and there was a spectacular vertical bluff across the creek which rose perhaps 80 to 100 feet. My first duty as a big-time adventurer was to drag out all the ancient cookware and eating utensils from the shack. My job was to carry them to the creek and scrub them clean. While that may have been a questionable "privilege," I tackled the task with great enthusiasm. I wanted to get into those woods A.S.A.P.

The trip was a success beyond my wildest imagination. Over the three or four day hunt, I not only saw my first wild whitetail deer, I may have seen 50 or more.

The woods were filled with wild turkey, bobcats, coyotes, and small game of all descriptions. To say I was smitten would be a grand understatement. Much to my surprise, and to my satisfaction, many of the things I had learned during my tamer excursions were quite applicable in the big woods as well. More importantly, I was given a broader perspective on the wild world at large. I was lucky to be there.

It was to my great benefit that I also got to meet several very experienced and knowledgeable woodsmen, out of the group of about 10 men who gathered at the camp. The sharing of duties, the helpful assistance, the careful instruction, and explanations about guns, hunting and ethical issues, were all an important part of the experience. It was my first taste of the flavor of a classic deer camp, with all its camaraderie, good-natured kidding and the really great tasting food. Of course, anything might have tasted good up on cloud nine, where I was sitting.

This was my first real introduction to the white-tailed deer, and I was impressed beyond words. Ever since that first trip, whitetails and their environments have been the embodiment of all that is truly wild and mysterious in nature to me.

I was invited back to that original deer camp a couple more times before it disbanded for reasons unknown. By then, I was an avowed whitetail "nut." Because of the fact that I didn't live in good whitetail country, and since I was somewhat economically challenged, my ability to walk among the whitetails was limited. For many years I had to be satisfied with a once-a-year adventure to the beloved deer woods far away. Nevertheless, I was intense about it, and my years were measured more from deer season to deer season than by other dates on the calendar. I dearly loved the time I spent in the environs of the deer.

In time, I (more or less) grew up, went to college, and took a flying leap into the hectic world of corporate America. I later became self-employed and had a couple of different types of businesses over the years. All along the way, I still managed to get into the wilds of the whitetail a few times each year. As I got older, the woods became a haven, as much as an adventure. Time passed, and after years of hard work and long hours, I stepped back to take a look, as many do, at age forty.

When I took a look at the big picture, the decision wasn't really that hard. No doubt the memories of that first deer camp, 29 years earlier, played some part in it. After due consideration, I decided that, one way or another, I would become professionally involved in the outdoors world, preferably with whitetail deer. The most appealing approach seemed to be through commercial wildlife photography and writing.

In truth, I knew just enough about photography of any kind to be dangerous and even less about writing. I had only bought my first camera a few years earlier, along with a cheap telephoto lens. I had used it as an excuse to make extra, early trips to the deer lease, in order to scout the area and hunt with my camera. In doing so, I had surprised the other members of the deer camp by showing them photos of whitetails which amazed them. They couldn't believe that those bucks were actually on our property.

Even though I probably should have known better, I decided that I **would** be a professional wildlife photographer. I would do whatever it took to learn the necessary skills. **It took a lot!** The other professional photographers weren't kidding when they told me in the beginning that it was very nearly impossible to make a living as a wildlife photographer. I do love the field work, but it is a brutally difficult way to make a living.

I set out to do the best job I could do. It may sound a bit stodgy, but I've always believed that if you're going to do a job at all, you should do it well. Initially, there were almost insurmountable odds to be overcome. There were countless questions about equipment, film and basic techniques, which had to be dealt with, before the real work could even begin. I'll always be grateful to some of the other pros, such as Wyman Meinzer, Jerry Smith and Grady Allen, for sharing some of their hard-earned experience with me way back when I hardly knew an F-stop from a door-stop.

Beyond that, I've worked as hard as I knew how, for the last nine years, to produce the best whitetail photography possible. Patience, persistence and trial-and-error have been my best teachers. I've learned that to be relentless in my efforts is to **occasionally** be successful with whitetail photography. I've watched many an empty meadow, after great expenditures of time and effort but I've also witnessed incredible scenes, filled with drama and suspense that I could never have imagined. I've learned a great deal about whitetails, after literally thousands of hours in the field with them, but they never cease to amaze me.

After having over 4,000 of my photos published, with something over 500 magazine and book covers, I decided to make this presentation on whitetails which I hope you will find to be unique and interesting. This book contains well over 300 full-color photos, illustrating what I believe are some of the most exciting moments ever photographed in the whitetail world. There are at least 250 different bucks pictured, and over 90% of the photography was accomplished in the wild. No matter what your experience level, I believe there will be some surprises in store for you. I hope you'll enjoy the views.

The quality of a woods or wilderness might be judged by the relative abundance or scarcity of white-tailed deer. A woods with whitetails is a magical, mystical place, but without the knowledge that big-racked bucks are prowling in the shadows, a wild place loses much of its magic. The beauty and mystique of the whitetail, once experienced, will never be forgotten.

THE CALL OF THE WHITETAIL

The unexpected sight of a mature whitetail buck such as this one, along with a silent sunrise streaking through early morning haze and fog will pick you up and whisk you away. If you had been there on the November morning when I took this photograph, you would have heard "The Call." There were no audible sounds to speak of, but "The Call" was loud and clear.

The elusive white-tailed deer is one of the most mysterious and alluring animals on the planet. With their secretive nature, their lives are full of surprises — with fascinating social behaviors and communication skills. Their grace and agility is remarkable, and their ability to appear and disappear, seemingly at will, is legendary. Above all else, man has always been mesmerized by their phenomenal antlers.

Whitetails have long been revered by humans, probably ever since some early hominid saw his first whitetail buck ages ago. They're still greatly admired by the modern humans fortunate enough to see

Whitetails in motion are like spirits in the wind. I surprised these two big bucks bedded on a hillside overlooking some farm country during a late morning hike. They were over the hill and out of sight within seconds. Whitetails frequently appear with little or no warning, and from places where you didn't expect them to be. Their elusive nature provides one surprise after another.

This handsome buck is in the process of shedding the velvet from his new antlers, in early September. Sometimes, a few shreds of velvet may hang on for several days.

them. In some ways the whitetail is a common bond between ourselves and the ancient hunters. Whitetails were a basic element in their lives for countless generations, and they're still an important element in many of our lives today. To experience the whitetail today is to share important personal experiences with many people over broad expanses of time.

From prehistoric times right on through much of American history, whitetails were almost essential — one of the necessities of life in those times. They provided food, clothing, and tools for the ancient hunters, the Indians, and the early settlers of America. No doubt there have been many times when the acquisition of a whitetail deer made the difference between eating or going hungry — perhaps even life or death.

There was a period in early America when market hunters saw the whitetail through the eyes of economic supply and

It was a cold fall morning, just a few minutes after sunrise, when I watched this heavy-antlered 11-point buck work his scrape line along the edge of a brushy creek. The big buck blowing "smoke" while he slipped along in the fog was a magical picture. He stopped to work over his "licking branches" and paw the ground on three separate occasions before he went out of sight.

demand. With burgeoning human populations in the cities came a high demand for venison, from people who wanted the meat, but who lacked the ability or the desire to get it on their own. Overall, this was a dark era for whitetails, as they were over-harvested in huge numbers, with little or no regard for their long-range management as a resource. There were no game laws or restrictions to speak of, and professional hunters became very efficient at their job. They simply viewed it as a livelihood. Unfortunately they were looking only at the short term, considering no provisions whatever for the future.

By the early 1900s, the once numerous whitetails had reached alarmingly low population levels throughout the country. What once had been a seemingly unlimited herd of many millions had been reduced to an estimated four or five hundred thousand animals. Market hunting declined with the dwindling supply of animals. A few forward thinking individuals finally realized the plight of the species. Game laws were passed and put into service, but the recovery of the decimated whitetail populations was slow. Even with game laws in effect, there was very little funding for enforcement, or for research to study the needs of the species.

Then, along the way, attitudes began to change. People in general began to become more conservation minded and sport hunting began to grow in popularity. As sport hunting has grown, the much needed funding for the enforcement of game laws, habitat improvement, and research has grown

These three bucks, still in a bachelor group in early fall, were crossing an open area in the dense fog when a nearby coyote burst into song, startling them. While coyotes are certainly responsible for some predation on deer, most healthy, mature deer are simply beyond their grasp, and these bucks had nothing to fear. They were just surprised by the sudden, unexpected howling.

Deep woods and deer! What a combination. This very respectable buck has just seen me as I was trying to slip through the woods on a dark, foggy, drizzly morning. He moved out quickly with his white flag waving goodbye. He was out of sight in another four or five seconds. As careful as I was, he probably saw me long before I saw him, but didn't bolt until I got too close.

tremendously. Through the sales of hunting licenses and a multitude of efforts on the part of sportsmen and sportsmen's groups, a massive nationwide wildlife management and conservation effort emerged.

Currently whitetail deer herds throughout North America have reached what may be the highest population numbers in their history, due largely to the interest of sport hunters. With the high levels of interest have come extensive research and management programs. Whitetails are being managed and studied like never before, to the mutual advantages of hunters and non-hunting nature lovers alike.

It's easy to see why so many people have become enthralled by the whitetail. In today's hectic and increasingly urbanized world, many people have lost touch with the natural world. Increasingly, many would like to touch it again, and the whitetail deer offers unique and satisfying opportunities to make that connection.

As modern men and women, whether hunters, photographers, or simply observers, find themselves in the presence of whitetail deer, they can momentarily see the world through the eyes of their predecessors. The hunting of whitetails — whether with gun, bow, camera, or binoculars — is a wonderful way to transport yourself to an earlier time and place. The process is a most effective "time machine." As card carrying members of the natural world, there's probably not a human among us who doesn't harbor at least a little of the ancient hunter deep inside. It's as natural as the sun rising.

This photo was taken in September ....the 13 point buck on the left is still in velvet ....the 10 pointer on the right has just shed his velvet. Silhouetted together, against the orange and golden rays of sunrise, the two mature bucks made an impressive sight.

In addition to the early hunter's genes, we also carry an ages-old appreciation for the aesthetics surrounding the whitetail. His world is a visual smorgasbord, filled with the colors of the seasons, the magic of antlers, and endless exhibitions of speed, grace and beauty. The early hunters commemorated their special encounters with pictographs and carved petroglyphs on the walls of caves. We still celebrate such encounters today with treasured photographs, paintings, carvings, bronzes, literature and so on. Many images experienced in the world of the whitetail are just so spectacular that we want to preserve them and share the wonder with others.

The vision of a big whitetail buck gliding silently through the swirling mists of a foggy November dawn is a profoundly moving experience. The sight of a muscled-up buck chasing a doe in the golden light of sunrise, is a view of poetry in motion. To observe the complex social behaviors in groups of whitetails is to be fascinated and amazed. If you're lucky enough to see some of the rarer sights, such as a fight for dominance between two mature bucks, that sight picture will stay with you for the rest of your days. In contrast to the violence of dominance battles, the picture of a doe and her fawn coming to water at sundown is the essence of peace and tranquility, and that too is a scene you'll remember.

The allure of the whitetail is strong. To those of us who walk among them, the

In late April, 100 days before this photo was taken, these bucks would have had virtually no antlers at all. Now, in August, the antlers are essentially full-grown. Antlers are the fastest growing bones in the world, and it's an amazing process, from start to finish.

Whitetails generally move around more, and are more visible, during the early morning or late afternoon hours ....especially in warmer weather. The dramatic lighting conditions of these times of the day contribute to many mystical whitetail scenarios.

This is a 6x7 ....13 point "typical" buck, a rarely seen antler configuration. He looked as though he was carrying a picket fence on his head as he ran down the edge of the brushline.

whitetail actually is much more than just a symbol of the wilderness. To the people who live in whitetail country, and those who visit it often — to those who truly love these animals — wildness and wilderness areas are defined by the presence of whitetails. The quality of a woods could well be judged by the relative abundance or scarcity of deer. A woods without whitetails would lose much of its magic, and without the knowledge of big-racked bucks prowling in the shadows, it might lose its sense of wildness altogether. The call of the whitetail, however silent, is both mystical and powerful. Once experienced, it will draw you back time and time again.

This wide, heavy-antlered drop-tine buck had no idea that I was hiding in a blind next to his afternoon watering hole. Seeing a monster buck coming straight at you like this is enough to rattle your nerves, no matter how many big deer you've seen before.

Some folks think that whitetails aren't "intelligent". Call it what you will ....This mature buck is certainly sizing up some type of situation. He is very alert, and in the process of collecting information with his nose, eyes and ears. Based on his experiences, he is about to make a decision, and the odds are that it's likely to be a good one, where his own best interests are concerned.

WHITETAIL "INTELLIGENCE"

Whitetails are constantly checking their surroundings, ever alert to the slightest change, whether it be sight, sound or smell. They regularly evaluate the situation behind them, as well as in front of them. Their ability to react quickly and intelligently is remarkable. Chasing after whitetails will definitely alter your perception of intelligence ...yours as well as theirs.

The American Heritage Dictionary defines "intelligence" as, "the capacity to acquire and apply knowledge." By this definition, whitetails are highly intelligent beings indeed. With their keenly developed sensory abilities, they are able to acquire and process detailed knowledge of their surroundings with incredible speed and accuracy. Add to this, their ability to learn, their capacity for memory and their quick and decisive nature, and the result is very impressive.

Whitetails can easily detect and identify odors that a human would never even be aware of. They are able to hear and interpret sounds that we would never hear at all. While their visual abilities aren't nearly as extravagant as their other sensory perceptions, their ability to detect even the smallest movement, at great distances, is legendary. Their ability to acquire sensory information, and to interpret it, is nothing less than amazing.

There is ample evidence that whitetails do learn from their experiences. You don't

This gorgeous buck with the huge swollen neck was working his way through the woods in search of a doe. He was working a scrape on this spot when he sensed my presence.

have to observe or hunt whitetails for very long to see that they learn very quickly, from both positive and negative factors. For example, a positive factor might be the offering of food for wild deer to eat, perhaps apples or corn. It is surprising how quickly deer will find the food, whether it is placed in an obvious situation or not. Further, after very few repetitions, maybe only two, the deer will be there at feeding time just like clockwork. It is quite common in spots where whitetails are fed supplementally with automatic feeders, with set timers, for the whitetails to show up just a couple of minutes before it's time for the feeder to go off. There will not have been a deer in sight for hours, when suddenly, several may show up within a three- or four-minute time period, in anticipation of the exact time that the feeder goes off each day.

An example of a negative learning experience might be in the way that whitetails respond to deer decoys, after only one previous experience. With today's life-like decoys, the visual cue is so strong that the majority of whitetails will be curious and want to investigate the "new" deer the first time they see it. However, once a particular whitetail has approached a given decoy, and found it to be unreceptive and phony, that deer is almost certain to ignore the decoy if it is used again on another day — even in a different spot. He will remember his experience and act as though the decoy doesn't even exist, in most cases.

Whitetails have a very accurate, highly detailed memory capacity. This has been illustrated for me on many occasions. A good example comes to mind. I was preparing an area for some serious whitetail photography. In order to produce really clean, publishable pho-

I saw this buck from a distance as he traveled across some very rough country, filled with deep ravines and heavy brush. Knowing the area quite well, I circled around and guessed which trail he might be taking. This shot was a split second opportunity, as he came out of a ravine to see me squatting in the trail 10 yards away with my camera. He just about turned inside-out.

Whitetails are incredibly adaptable animals, easily adjusting to the intrusion of farming activities. They are likely to partake of the crops, drink with the livestock, and sleep in the fencerows.

tographs, a great deal of thought must go into the backgrounds as well as the subjects themselves. During the middle of the day, I had cleaned up the area in front of my blind, in anticipation of photographing deer traveling down a well-used trail which went right through the middle of a small open area. I removed a small amount of debris, such as particularly unsightly rocks and sticks. Late that afternoon, the deer began moving. On several occasions deer were coming down the trail, just as I had hoped they would. However, each deer, as they reached a certain spot, would suddenly stop. At that point, they would exhibit a variety of different "alarm" behaviors ...neck-stretching, stomping, blowing, etc. Then the deer would spook and run away.

I could not figure out what they were afraid of. From my position in the blind, there was nothing visible at that spot but grass, but whatever it was, something was obviously very disturbing to the deer coming down that trail.

When darkness finally came, I was totally frustrated. I had seen three different bucks coming down that trail which would have been great photo subjects, but each one had spooked and fled when they came to the "scary" spot.

When I came out of my blind, I went directly to the spot. At first I could see absolutely nothing that would cause such behavior. Then, studying the situation further, I realized that while cleaning up the area for photography, I had moved a small dead log that was sticking up out of the grass at an unsightly

In many areas, whitetail populations have grown to such an extent as to create hazardous driving conditions, particularly at night and/or during the rut.

angle. It had only been moved about 8 or 10 feet. However, I inadvertently had pitched it right across the deer trail which crossed the clearing.

It was only a small log, perhaps five inches in diameter, but to the deer coming down that trail, it might as well have been a giant sequoia! These deer knew, and remembered, their environment on a very detailed basis. They knew, when they saw that log in the trail, that something had changed. While it seems a little extreme that they would run away from a log which posed no danger, it should be taken into account that due to hunting and other activities on the ranch, the deer were probably somewhat spooky to begin with. The log itself posed no danger, but it was an indicator of change. Until cautious whitetails have had time and opportunity to

In suburban and rural areas, where there are substantial populations of whitetails, it is often quite common for whitetails to live in fairly close quarters with humans, frequenting yards and gardens at night or when the people are not present ...and sometimes even when they are. It can sometimes become a considerable problem, as the deer eat the flowers and shrubs from the yards.

Whitetails in suburban environments are becoming more common in many parts of the country. It's not known whether or not they adhere to the posted speed limits.

thoroughly investigate any change in their environment, they tend to regard the change itself as a threat.

I experienced yet another particularly remarkable example of whitetail memory and sensory perception. I had set up to try to rattle up some whitetail bucks for photography. It was a totally wild situation, and the setting was a large block of dense, old-growth forest. I was fully camouflaged and had set up at a crossing of two old unused roads which had been cut through the woods many years before. All things considered, it was a very successful morning, as I rattled in eight different bucks at that one location on a drizzly, foggy November morning. The rut was in full

swing, and three of the bucks had been quite substantial.

The last buck to come in was a really nice high-tined eight pointer. He spotted me and ran, but came back when I rattled the antlers again. After watching me for several minutes, he became more casual about my presence, eventually just walking away. When he got about 80 or 90 yards away, I decided that I would try going after him, to try for more photographs. He was very photogenic, and since he was leaving, I really had nothing to lose. I had pretty well used up that rattling location by then.

I was carrying two large cameras, one on a tripod, which were also fully camouflaged. As I began walking toward him, not really trying to hide as that would have been impossible, he showed some concern, but was not overly fearful. As I followed behind him, I moved very slowly, and tried

Whitetails are often very curious animals. This is a wild buck checking out a large brushpile fire. He approached from a considerable distance to study the fire.

Whitetails are one of the few large animals that can be at home in either remote woods or in areas with human development, assuming there is some food and cover present. They are highly adaptable to a variety of situations. Easily the biggest danger posed to the well-being of whitetails is the overall destruction of habitat. Adaptable as they are, they must have food and cover to survive.

Whitetails have learned to live with all kinds of other animals, including many of the exotic deer which have been brought in to various parts of the country. This wild whitetail is sharing space with an Axis deer, who has recently shed his antlers and has just begun to grow new ones. Axis deer may shed and regrow their antlers at almost any time of the year, depending on the individual.

I was driving through a ranch late one morning and I almost didn't notice this very large, wild buck among a large flock of sheep. Sheep were kept on the ranch on a regular basis, and the buck had adapted to living with them.

to assume a non-threatening posture as much as possible. As I began to close the gap between us, I walked in random directions and only looked at him obliquely, not wanting him to feel that he was being pursued. I became nothing more than another animal in the woods, calm, non-threatening and generally going about my own business. Of course, coincidentally, I was getting closer and closer to him as we made our way along. After about an hour of this, I was ambling along in the woods within 20 to 25 yards of a completely wild whitetail buck — a remarkable situation! When he would stop, I would also stop, or make a step or two in the other direction. Occasionally, I would get too close for comfort, or I might accidentally snap a twig, and he would jump out there another 20 yards or so. As I kept

This whitetail has become so accustomed to farming activity that he pays no mind at all to the farm tractor plowing the field only 150 yards from where he stands in the open. He's much more interested in a doe which he is watching in the distance.

a close watch on his body language for clues as to his alarm status, I would take a quick photo or two every time I saw an opportunity.

I followed him through woods and across creeks for perhaps three hours, as he worked his scrape line. Suddenly, he stopped abruptly about 30 yards ahead. He stretched his head high and every muscle in his body became tense. I couldn't figure out what it was that upset him so. I thought perhaps it was another deer which I had not yet seen, or maybe a predator of some type. We were deep into the heavy timber.

The buck stared to the left, tense and alert, for several long minutes, then he finally seemed to relax and continued

Whitetails have no qualms about drinking out of livestock water troughs, although more times than not they'll do it under cover of darkness. In dry areas, they depend on such sources.

Whitetails regularly take advantage of domestic water supplies on farms and ranches, especially during dry years. This mature buck has had to wade into the mud to get to the shrinking water hole.

his travels. Even after I reached the spot where he had stopped, it took a while to figure out what the problem was. When I finally saw it, I was amazed. About 80 yards to the left, through the weeds and the brush and the timber, sat my camouflaged camera and tripod, next to a tree. A couple of hours earlier it had become too cumbersome to carry through the tangled woods and I had left it to be retrieved later. We had been traveling in large circles through the woods and had come back close to our earlier route. The camouflaged camera and tripod were motionless, low to the ground, and partially

This group of deer was caught out in an open crop field, just after sunrise on a cold October morning. No doubt they were regularly taking advantage of the situation. In a dry season such as this was, with a shortage of wild browse and forbs, food plots and croplands will draw deer from all around the countryside, concentrating many deer into a relatively small area.

Adaptable whitetails learn to live with and work around many manmade structures. They have been known to bed down in barns and cellars, and they regularly drink out of livestock water troughs in many places. Normal walls and fences on farms and ranches rarely impede their travel patterns. In fact, they learn to use the cover of fencerows to their advantage in traveling around farms.

hidden behind brush and weeds 80 yards away! Yet, the buck had stopped as though someone was shouting and flashing neon lights at him! I'm still amazed by it. The camera was very difficult to see, even after I found it. This whitetail obviously knew his territory intimately, and the way he remembered it, this small foreign object didn't belong there. It represented a change, and as previously mentioned, a change is taken as a threat until it has been considered and/or investigated thoroughly.

Many fence crossings are made in this simple, easy way. I've seen all manner of big bucks go under extremely low fences with ease. Only rarely, will a big buck have difficulty fitting his antlers under the bottom wire.

Whitetails are frequently found in the vicinity of railroad tracks. The creation of open edges when the right-of-way was cut through the woods provides edge habitat and food for the deer.

(Incidentally, I walked with this wild buck for over FIVE hours, practically non-stop from 8:30 a.m. until after 1:30 p.m. Had he not been so pre-occupied with the rut and his scrape line, it might not have been possible. At any rate, it was one of the most interesting and educational whitetail classes I've ever attended. In the end, the big eight pointer bedded down against a tree about 20 yards from me. I left, exhausted and out of film, and I was never able to find that particular buck again. The photograph on page 31 is one of the photos I took while following him.)

We've read and heard for years that a whitetail is intimately familiar with his territory. Based on these examples, and many others which I have witnessed, I think it would be hard to over-estimate that familiarity. In the abode of the whitetail, very little goes unnoticed.

Not only do whitetails remember WELL, they also remember LONG. I've seen some situations where I was really surprised by their long-term memory. There have been a number of ranches and other places over the years where I have fed the deer in order to attract them to an area for photography — places where they were not accustomed to being fed. Although what I'm about to describe has occurred in several of these places, there is one incident in particular that stands out.

It was a fairly large ranch on which the whitetails were not fed or baited. Beginning late one summer, I would drive back into the ranch in my truck, and feed the deer on a semi-regular basis. I was always in the same truck and I intentionally made a lot of noise when I went out to deliver the feed (corn, which they love). I literally called them, hollered for them, rattled the

On ranches and farms which have a lot of cross-fencing, most fences don't pose much of a problem. If the bottom portion is hog-wire or goat-wire, the whitetails simply jump over. They go from pasture to pasture like you might go from room to room.

bucket as loudly as possible, beat on the door of the truck, and did every thing I could to make the deer associate my presence with the delivery of their favorite food. After a couple of months, I was able to approach the deer in my truck, and photograph them at quite close ranges. By the beginning of winter, some of the deer would come running toward the truck whenever they could see or hear it.

After the end of the year, due to other work obligations, I didn't return to the ranch for several months. In fact, it was about eight months before I got back there during the next August. I drove back into the ranch fairly quietly about daybreak. Out of curiosity, as to whether or not anything would happen, I began by only calling aloud for the deer as I had done the year before. Almost immediately after I began hollering, three bucks came running over the hill, directly towards me. They had not seen or heard me in eight months. Not

I was walking along the edge of a creek when I jumped this buck. He used the old wooden bridge to cross the creek, instead of the more traditional method.

I had been in a deer blind watching this mature buck "guarding" this particular doe for over an hour, when the coyote appeared about 500 yards down the open lane. The coyote came closer and closer, and finally approached the two deer directly. At that time the buck took the offensive, lowering his antlers and charging at the coyote until the coyote fled.

Whitetails normally flee in terror when approached by feral hogs of ANY size. The very idea that a buck would even consider facing down this gargantuan porker is contrary to all reason. While the buck is not a small animal, perhaps 200 pounds or so ....the hog appears to be at least 500 pounds. Just after this photo was taken, the buck turned and casually walked away.

In the courses of their lives, whitetails co-exist with, and cross the paths of, a wide diversity of other creatures. Generally speaking, they are pacifists, practicing avoidance and compromise, where space is concerned. However, on a given day, they can be prone to having an "attitude," just like other animals. This buck literally "charged" the wild turkey and ran him off the hillside.

Are these reactions borne out of curiosity? Or are they acts of defiance, rooted in territorial dominance? Perhaps a little of both. While whitetails usually avoid or ignore the other animals with whom they share their environment, there are occasions where they become curious and others when they can be quite aggressive. Each day is a new day, as this javelina is finding out.

A whitetail's ears can be rotated, turned, and cupped in almost all directions, in order to key in on any suspicious sounds. They can be aimed in two different directions simultaneously.

Curiosity seems to be getting the better of this small yearling buck. He just doesn't know what to think about the armadillo. Whitetails are constantly checking out their surroundings.

This buck has detected an odor in the air. He's really trying to concentrate the smell in his nostrils, to analyze it further. A whitetail lives by his nose.

only did they remember, they seemed to remember very enthusiastically. Shortly thereafter, two more deer came out of the brushline and headed for the truck.

Now, after having worked on the ranch sporadically for a number of years, there have been a couple of times when I've been absent from the place for a year or more. Nevertheless, whenever I travel to that ranch, the deer always seem to remember, whether the last trip was a week ago or a year ago.

Any way you look at it, when you mix a whitetail's incredible sensory abilities, with a very quick learning curve and include a detailed, long-term memory, you've got an impressive base to work from. Next, pitch in a well-tuned batch of instinctive traits, a remarkable will to survive, and the ability to react on a split-second basis, and you have an animal which is able to deal with a wide variety of problems and situations, in

It's hard enough to slip past, or sneak up on, a solitary white-tail. It's even more difficult to go unnoticed when there are several together. As you can imagine from these two separate examples, very little gets past 6 eyes, 6 ears, and 3 noses.

The safety-in-numbers concept works well for whitetails during the times when they are grouped together. However slight the noise, or the movement, or the odor, there will almost always be one in the group who will notice and warn the others — by snorting, stomping, tail flaring or running.

This nice 11-point buck was caught out in the open, 300 yards from the nearest cover, on a very foggy October morning. Had it not been for the greatly reduced visibility, I probably would never have gotten this close before he spooked. Even though whitetails can see through the fog much better than we can, it does decrease overall visibility, and evens up the odds just a little bit. Sometimes, it also seems to give them a false sense of security.

Whitetails are ever alert to the dynamics of their surroundings. Their ability to see, hear and smell gives them a huge amount of information as to what is going on around them.

a very intelligent and effective manner. Whitetails are able to cope with changes and challenges in their environment very effectively — perhaps as well as any other large wild animal.

Partly as a result of their "intelligence," whitetails have become one of the most adaptable large animals on earth. As previously described, they are extremely cautious animals by nature. They will not willingly rush headlong into any new situation or environment. At the same time, they are very curious animals, and given the opportunity to investigate new situations **on their own terms**, they'll frequently adjust their behaviors and living patterns to better relate to the new situation.

Whitetails were originally woodland animals. However, over the years, as they have expanded their ranges in search of food and habitat, they have adapted to all kinds of circumstances. They still live in the woodlands and bottomlands, but also prosper in the broken cover of the midwestern plains and the foothills of the Rockies. They do extremely well in farming country and on many ranch lands. Some of the most impressive whitetails in the world live in the arid southwestern part of Texas and northern Mexico, where drought is the norm, and summer temperatures commonly exceed 100 degrees F. They make much of their living off such foods as guajillo, blackbrush and prickly pear. At the same time, whitetails of the northern American states and Canada, living through the harsh cold of the sub-zero winters have evolved into enormous-bodied animals, with impressive antlers as well, living off such items as white cedar, ground hemlock and maple. Whitetails in all kinds of extreme situations have learned to cope with the challenges of their respective areas. Wherever they live, they seem to make the most of the available food, cover and other resources.

Far and away, the most serious threat to whitetails everywhere is the relentless expansion of human populations, and the concurrent destruction of habitat that comes with land development. As human populations spread out and lands are cleared, whitetails are forced to move to less productive, poorer habitats. Such encroachment has dramatically limited, if not doomed, many animal species, such as the wolves, bears, and bison, just to name a few. However, so far, the whitetail has been able to move, adjust, and prosper far more successfully than any other large wild animal. This is not to say that every story is a success story, but the amount of success is very impressive indeed.

The whitetail's ability to survive, and succeed, in a constantly changing environment is a remarkable accomplishment for the species. While these cautious animals are often thought of as shy and timid, they are also exceedingly tenacious where survival is concerned, both as a species and as individuals. When it comes to survival, they may well turn and fight a wolf or a coyote. If it's called for, they will attempt to jump an eight-foot wall, or swim across a mile-wide lake.

Among all their other challenges, whitetails are also subject to disease, injury, and starvation, just like any other animal. Here too, while they obviously are not always successful, they are incredibly tenacious. No doubt many injuries, whether accidental or predator-induced, are fatal in an environment where the body must heal itself, or else. Nevertheless, many

Whitetails know their home environment intimately. They seem to know every tree, bush, twig and leaf. If anything is new or different in any way, they usually know it instantly.

The buck on the left has completely lost the ankle and hoof off his left rear leg. When walking, he hopped like a jackrabbit, but he could run surprisingly well. He survived at least two years like this that I know of, even though there was a large population of predators in the area. The buck on the right has a condition called "lumpy jaw." It's generally caused by the compacting of food beneath broken-down gums. It is just one of many ailments that whitetails occasionally have to face in their constant battle for survival.

Whitetails are subject to all kinds of injuries, some serious, some perhaps only embarrassing. The buck on the left, photographed in April, has broken his left front leg, and it has healed incorrectly, leaving him with a club foot. I saw him again the following year, and he walked and ran normally. The buck in the middle literally has no tail, reason unknown. I've since seen another buck elsewhere which also had no tail. Perhaps the tails were ripped off by coyotes? Who knows? The doe on the right is badly crippled. Her left front leg seems to have broken at the knee, and then healed at an awkward crooked angle.

I came across this poor buck on the left on a late October afternoon. He had injured his jaw and ear and had developed a terrible infection. He was so sick that he had not even lost his velvet. I doubt that he survived much longer. The buck on the right is an interesting deer. Besides having small drop-tines on each beam, and double brow tines, he also has a deep, wide, foot-long scar on his back, probably from fighting during the previous year.

whitetails seem to cope very well with illness and injury. Some live for years with abnormal growths, or crooked legs which have broken and healed incorrectly. I've seen many bucks with major scars, and occasionally puncture wounds, which are testament to the extreme violence of dominance battles. I've observed two one-eyed deer, and three three-legged bucks in the wild, all of which seemed to be functioning extremely well under the circumstances.

I saw one of the three-legged bucks again about a year after the first sighting, and he was not only still alive, but seemed to be in better shape than the year before. This in an environment teeming with coyotes and other predators. The old boy hobbled around and hopped like a jackrabbit when he was walking, but I once had occasion to see him spook and run. After the first step or two, he was able to run at a high rate of speed, seemingly just as fleet

of foot as any other whitetail. Another buck which I observed only once had a grotesquely crooked neck which apparently had been broken and healed at an awkward angle. I thought it remarkable that a wild deer would survive a broken neck.

There are apparently an incredible number of terrible situations in which whitetails not only survive, but actually cope with pretty well. I know some people with a farm in central Texas who accidentally hit a baby fawn while mowing hay one summer. The fawn's front legs were both taken off at the knees, yet he ran away on the stubs, assumedly to die. Amazingly, the fawn survived, and grew to be a substantial mature buck, as the years went by. Goodness knows, he was easy enough to identify, with his lowered front end. When it comes to survival, whitetails are incredibly resilient and tenacious animals.

The buck on the right was actually the original aggressor here, but when he tried to intimidate the other buck he got more than he bargained for. The buck on the left turned out to be the more dominant one. He is about to whack the first one in the face with his front hooves. The buck on the right has his eyes closed in anticipation of getting hit. The next blow knocked him sideways.

WHITETAIL BEHAVIOR

Whitetails, in establishing and maintaining their social order and dominance structure, perform a wide variety of behaviors. Observing and understanding the nuances of these behaviors will vastly increase your ability to predict their movements and activities. Some of the behaviors are so dramatic that you may get an entirely new perspective on America's favorite big game animal.

The white-tailed deer is surely one of the most wonderfully enigmatic creatures on earth. While viewed by many as the essence of peace and tranquility in nature, the whitetail's moods can swing like a pendulum, and a very fast moving one at that. He can make the transition from peaceful serenity, to high-speed action — or even to obscene violence — in the blink of an eye, or the stomp of a hoof. In one moment you may be looking at the perfect picture of beauty, grace, and harmony. In the next moment, as though somebody switched channels, you see an entirely different scenario.

Whitetails can't really help it. It's the way they are put together — the way whitetail social structure has been defined and maintained for eons. Every whitetail is simply "born to be bad" under certain sets of circumstances. It is the only method that a whitetail has, to establish and maintain status in a complex social hierarchy.

Whitetail social structure is based upon the relative dominance of the individual animals which make up the "herd" in any given area. This "dominance factor" is an extremely powerful force. It is the thread which holds together the fabric of whitetail society and creates a continuity within the herd. It defines authority, and creates

Most of the year, the does live pretty much separately from the bucks. The most basic social units among whitetails are the various doe-groups, which may contain mothers and daughters, and last year's fawns. Bucks may cross paths with the various doe-groups during the year, but they rarely spend much time around them ...except of course, during the rut.

You will usually find the widest mixture of animals and age groups together in association with food sources or water. This group of various-aged bucks was caught out in the open, feeding in a farm field.

order. The acting out of dominance behaviors is constantly rearranging the social hierarchies, creating a steadily improving ability of the species to cope with social pressures within the herd as well as outside factors. This continuing process carries out the whitetail version of "survival of the fittest."

Only those animals who are able to cope with and survive the pressures of the outside factors are then able to compete within the herd. Consequently the most successful and dominant animals rise to the top of the social structure. A whitetail's command of dominant tendencies will dictate the success of that animal's social skills, and will determine social standing within the herd. It will greatly affect the extent of a buck's contribution to the gene pool, as well as the quality of his life in general.

In whitetail society, dominance is an incredibly powerful force in the lives of all whitetails — bucks, does, and fawns. For all deer there are essentially three primary driving forces in their lives. First, there is the need to survive. Second, is the need to reproduce and perpetuate the species. And third, is the need to dominate. Dominance is a much larger issue than you might imagine.

Whitetails begin working on their status in the social pecking order, or "dominance structure," at a very early age. They actually begin as spotted fawns. These yearling bucks will quickly become experienced players.

This is a rare, but not unheard of scenario. Since some of the other deer species have a dominance tendency which is somewhat similar to that of the whitetail, there will occasionally be a confrontation between different species. Both the Axis buck and the whitetail buck are yearlings and are engaging in a pushing match as though they were interacting with their own kind.

Whitetail does are frequently very aggressive among themselves. Each doe-group has a dominant head-mistress, who is more or less the leader of the group.

mental image of two bucks squaring off, and going head-to-head, with the winner being the buck which is the "oldest" or "biggest" or "best." These antler-to-antler battles do take place every fall and winter, and they can be very impressive. However, the winners are not necessarily the "oldest" or "biggest," and maybe not even the "best," depending upon your definition.

Among bucks, dominance is not based solely on antler size. In fact, antler size may have very little to do with it. Neither is it based singularly on age, body weight or physical strength. Dominance will be determined by a combination of all these factors, along with some degree of individual "intelligence" and experience. There is also one other very important element which comes into play. It could be referred to as "an attitude". It may well be that the victor in many whitetail dominance con-

The satisfaction of the other two primary needs is often facilitated by the dominance factor. The obvious need for survival is many times accomplished with the help of domination skills. For example, when food is scarce, the more dominant deer invariably will get the most or best food. Also, the accomplishment of reproduction and perpetuation of the species, is greatly enhanced by the dominance factor. As a generality, it is felt that the majority of breeding is done by the most dominant bucks. The whitetail's need to dominate is an incredibly strong drive and at times it seems to outweigh any concern for any other needs whatsoever.

In whitetail literature, much has been written about "dominant bucks." What quickly comes to mind for most people is a

Whitetail bucks are constantly "trying" each other, throughout the entire year. Even though the basic structure may be fairly well established, "rank" must constantly be defended.

Bucks almost always stand up and fight with their hooves when they are not carrying hard antlers on their heads. They don't want to damage their tender, soft antlers. The hard kicks with the sharp hooves are serious. You may be able to see all the hair floating in the air here, from the last volley of kicks.

Sometimes does are actually dominant over some bucks, as where you have a high-ranking doe and a low-ranking buck. The buck may be old, or he may be injured (which lowers his rank).

tests will be the one with the boldest "attitude." Naturally, in order to compete in the first place, it would be necessary for a buck to have achieved some minimum amount of physical stature.

The classic "buck-fight" certainly does come into play on occasion, but dominance in whitetail society is based on much more than just the clashing of

During the summertime, whitetail bucks form "bachelor groups". Sometimes the bucks in a group are all near the same age class but other times they include a mixture of age groups. A bachelor group may consist of only two bucks, but there are commonly three to five, and occasionally there are as many as a dozen or more bucks in the same group.

From the look on this big velvet buck's face, you can be certain that there is another buck nearby. This is called a "snort-wheeze" and is the ultimate insult from one whitetail to another.

antlers in the fall. Dominance contests actually take many different forms. Most times dominance is determined, or reinforced, by the projection of a visible "attitude" from one deer to another. There is an entire array of different approaches, postures, actions and reactions, which define these attitudes under various conditions and circumstances.

As an end result of all this dominance testing, dominant whitetails are those individual animals which achieve the highest social standing. They might be viewed as the ones who receive the most "respect" from the other whitetails. This process of establishing and maintaining the social hierarchy is not reserved only for the pre-rut and rut periods. These are simply the times when it's most obvious to hunters and observers, because these are the times when people are in the woods the most. It is actually a year-round, continuous process for all members of the whitetail community. Each individual has his or her niche in relation to all others in an immediate area. It is a constantly changing hierarchy, with challenges constantly being issued and answered. Some younger bucks will be dominant over some older bucks, some smaller bucks will be dominant over some larger bucks and some does will even be dominant over some bucks.

Throughout the year, various dominant behaviors can be observed in relation to "rights" to particular spots to feed, drink, bed or simply stand. The more dominant animals "own" the primary rights to the favored places and they will commonly move others out of the way. The dominance drive is so prominent that there are times when a dominant animal will seem to be exercising his "rank" for no particular reason at all, other than to reinforce the fact that he or she **IS** dominant. This reinforcement process goes on continuously, endlessly, day after day.

As mentioned, the most obvious dominance behavior to be observed is among bucks during the pre-rut and rut periods. While these bucks have

Dramatic stand-ups do not always result in a physical attack. They begin as a big "bluff," and as with many other kinds of whitetail posturing, the less-dominant animal will many times back off before the blows start flying.

This is an extremely rare sight ...two bucks in velvet, which are locking antlers. Bucks with velvet antlers virtually always avoid fighting with their tender antlers. This is the only time I've ever seen it.

As the summer comes to an end and early fall approaches, confrontations begin to take on a slightly more serious tone. The scene at the top of the page is a highly unusual one, in that the more dominant buck is still in velvet. Generally, once a buck removes his velvet, he is usually dominant over any buck which is still in velvet, assumedly because of his fighting advantage. In this case the velvet buck is backing down the hard-antlered buck. Both are very large, one is a 6x8 typical and the other is a 6x7. The other two photos show the increasing intensity of early fall standoffs. You can see which buck is dominant in each photo.

been participating in various dominance contests all year long, the physiological changes brought about by the season amplify their dominant tendencies substantially. With an overdose of testosterone boiling in their systems, they become very edgy and very intolerant of those who would dare to infringe upon any of their "rights" or "territories," either intentionally or by accident. A buck's "territory," where dominance is concerned, is the immediate area surrounding whatever location that buck happens to be in on a given day. In this respect, a buck takes his "territory" with him wherever he goes.

Dominant behaviors are carried out in many different fashions. Some are so subtle as to be almost imperceptible, while others are quite obvious. The performance of a dominance challenge is usually carried out in stages, or levels, with each succeeding stage escalating to a more serious threat than the preceding one. The first

It is very rare for whitetail bucks with hardened and polished antlers to stand up and kick-box, but apparently the bucks in both of these photos have forgotten that. In both cases the velvet just has been taken off the antlers and the bucks are more than likely simply following their habits of the last several months.

These photos show a very unusual situation, in which a young buck is poking an older deer in the neck, trying to pick a fight. The older buck, tried to ignore him, but when the small deer persisted, the older buck participated with him in a "sparring match." It seemed that the big deer was "letting" the small buck win, as though he might be contributing to the learning process in this way.

More times than not, it is the young to middle-aged bucks who participate in "sparring matches." The two bucks sparring in the forefront of this photo are nice deer, but probably only in the 2½ to 3½-year-old range. The mature buck in the background has taken a look, and decided that neither of these two is any real threat to his more dominant status and is turning away.

Dominant behavior is presented in many different fashions, some very subtle and others very obvious. These two deer, feeding on a hilltop at sunrise, would not seem to be in a highly competitive environment at the moment. However, the slightly heavier buck on the left felt the need to remind the other of his dominance, and his point seems to be well taken.

stage is commonly nothing more than a simple glance, even from a distance. Direct eye contact of any type is generally considered to be an affront. If the simple glance brings no reaction, the challenger may upgrade the threat to a hard stare — a definite insult. If there is still no response, or if the other animal returns the hard stare, one may move closer to the other, and go through the "glance" and "stare" stages again. As simple as it may seem, these "looks" that whitetails give each other are their most basic forms of interaction.

If these early stages don't provoke the preferred response, and if the participants are bucks, occasionally one of the bucks will walk confidently over to the nearest piece of brush, lower his antlers and literally tear it apart in an intimidation threat.

Sometimes it's a half-hearted effort, but many times it is extremely violent. I've seen more than one sizable buck leave the scene after such a display by a more dominant animal ...seeking safety at a high rate of speed. Observers take note. I've also seen other bucks coming in to investigate these violent displays. Accordingly, there are times when "busting brush" seems to work as well as or better than rattling antlers in attempting to bring deer in.

The brush-busting intimidation is only an occasional behavior among bucks. More times than not, if neither the "glance" nor the "stare" results in one or the other deer moving away in submission, then one or both may approach the other with the neck stretched as high as possible, trying to tower over the other. Occasionally one or

Going into the fall, as bucks begin to feel the effects of their increased testosterone levels, more and more fights start to break out. Still, the "fights" are usually carried out in the form of a "sparring match," and are rarely of a deadly nature. For the most part, they are precursors of fights-yet-to-be, or in many cases of fights-that-never-will-be, as they get the feel of each other's strength.

A direct stare like this is an obvious testing of the waters. The nearer buck, with his more flattened ears, is more dominant than the other, which shows a more tentative attitude

both will stand completely on their hind legs, and flail viciously at the other with the front hooves. Does "flail" fairly commonly but bucks do it only rarely. Flailing by bucks is confined almost entirely to the time periods when they have dropped their antlers, or when their antlers are in velvet.

If neither deer has yet backed away, the next stage will probably consist of a hard tensing of the neck muscles, with the ears severely flattened against the head, and if a buck, the antlers are lowered a little and presented. Also, many times the buck will cause his body hair to stand erect, which makes him appear larger. This can make the color of a buck seem to darken, almost to black. The dominant, or perhaps mutual approach is usually a stiff-legged, almost sideways approach, with the head cocked a bit to one side. As they approach each other in this fashion, along with a hard sideways stare, one of the deer will usually

As the fall progresses, the various threats and postures become ever more serious. While both of these bucks are mature, the big 11-pointer on the right is every bit the king-of-the-hill than he appears to be. His swollen neck and muscular stature are testament to age, experience and exercise. The attitude he is projecting with his ears, head, and body posture, is a deadly serious warning.

make a sudden run, or jump, at the other deer. Usually one or the other will lose their nerve and run away, showing their submission. If none of these stages have worked, and both deer are still at a "dominance" standoff, then, apparently there is going to be a physical confrontation ...and soon.

For bucks there is one final short performance called the "snort-wheeze." Along with a very severe hard stare, usually at fairly close range, a buck will let loose with several short, staccato, guttural blows or "snorts," followed by a long drawn-out "wheeze." The wheeze is made by sucking air back in through almost closed lips, which are contorted into an ugly sneer. This is the ultimate insult. Something is going to happen ...right now!

When bucks are in velvet antlers, they try to protect their tender antlers.

Generally speaking, a hard stare is a definite insult, or at the least, a challenge of authority. One or the other will submissively turn and move away or the threat will escalate.

This super wide-racked buck is "bustin' brush" in an effort to impress another buck which is nearby. If he is ferocious enough in his attack on the bush, the other buck may decide to take flight ...or at least turn around and leave, indicating submission. It's a macho act, which says: "If you mess with me, this is what I'll do to you." Sometimes it is very effective.

Sometimes when a buck is seriously threatening another, he will stand the hair up all over his body, which makes him appear larger. This heavy-bodied buck has almost turned black in the process. In the inset photo, taken a few seconds earlier as he "snort-wheezed," his appearance was much lighter in color.

Physical confrontation is carried out with merciless kicking and flailing with the sharp front hooves. Much of the time, they aim for the face, the neck, or the tender antlers. When bucks are in "hard antler," physical confrontation is carried out mostly by the clashing of antlers, and with much struggling, pushing and gasping. Each tries to force the other by brute strength into a submissive position.

There are really two completely different types of antler-to-antler fighting among whitetail bucks. The most common, by far, would more appropriately be called a sparring match. More times than not, it is the young or middle-aged bucks who participate in sparring matches. These are usually fairly light-duty pushing matches that may last for quite a while, but which are usually not especially violent. The other type of fighting is an unmistakably serious affair. It is extremely loud and violent, and is usually (but not always) a contest between two mature animals. Truly serious fights occur much, much less frequently than sparring matches. The vast majority of hunters and observers who come in and say that they have seen a "buck fight," have actually witnessed a sparring match. I've seen hundreds of "sparring matches," and they are always an interesting sight to see, but they're not the real thing. I've watched about 30 unmistakably serious battles, and each of them has left me breathless.

Bucks will also "bust brush" in the absence of other deer. It's their way of "working-out" — strengthening and fine-tuning their neck and shoulder muscles and practicing their fighting skills.

If you ever see a big, muscled-up buck coming toward you like this, it will be time to take cover or back away immediately. This unique view was taken with a telephoto lens over the shoulder of the buck he was threatening.

To watch two big bucks charge fearlessly into serious battle is a sight of a lifetime. The adrenaline flows, the eyes bulge, the muscles strain, and it's all-out war — no holds barred. They flip each other over by the antlers and they may try to broadside each other. On occasion, they break those incredibly strong antlers. They draw blood, break bones and occasionally lose eyes. It's a deadly serious business. If you are ever privileged to witness one of these knock-down, drag-outs, you'll likely be talking to yourself when it's over. It is maximum-strength drama.

The fact is, the various stages of assertive posturing and behavior are usually very effective in solving questions of dominance. Usually, during one of the earlier stages, the less dominant animal will react submissively and defer or move out of the way. Probably not one in a hundred

This confrontation between two heavy, mature bucks, had a very high violence potential. The timing is well into the pre-rut period and you can tell by looking at these two behemoths that they have both already begun working themselves into a frenzy. Just after this shot, the buck on the left, a 5x7 typical, arched his back and let loose with a severe "snort-wheeze." When the other buck, a 5x5, hesitated just a little, the 5x7 made a false jump at him ...and the 5x5 ran away in submission.

This buck is marching toward another buck with his chin up, his ears back and performing a "snort-wheeze." If all other posturing has not impressed the adversary into submission, the snort-wheeze is usually the last warning before a physical attack.

encounters actually results in a serious physical confrontation.

Perhaps the most useful knowledge we can gain by understanding the interactive behaviors of whitetails, is the overall ability to understand the body language of whitetails — both the subtle and the severe. Through considerable observation, and experience, you can learn to read the body language of the deer in front of you, to the extent that you can predict with a high degree of reliability what that deer will do next. You can predict to a reasonably accurate extent, which direction the deer will go and whether or not the movement will be fast or slow. Many times you will know when there is another unseen deer in the vicinity and in some cases,

This photo is one frame out of a deadly-serious fight between two mature bucks. It was an early morning in late November, and the fog was so thick, you could hardly see. It was much too dark for photography and the only way I managed to get this shot and a handful of others was to try to shoot with a super-slow shutter speed at the exact moment when they hit, hoping that they would be still for just an instant. The buck on the left has just broken off a 5-inch right brow tine within the last 10 seconds. About a minute previous, one of the bucks threw the other in the air and onto his back. It was a very dramatic fight that probably lasted about seven or eight minutes. The buck who lost his brow tine turned out to be the winner.

whether or not the unseen deer is a buck or a doe. The more deer you have in sight, the more knowledge you can have about what is going on, even beyond your range of visibility.

If you study the whitetail dominance factor, as well as all interactive whitetail behavior, it will make you a better hunter, or observer or photographer. You will understand much more about what makes a deer "tick", and you'll be able to predict deer movement much more accurately. There will be times when you will know what a buck is going to do, perhaps before he knows it himself.

I was watching this buck from the secrecy of a deer blind. While I never did see the other buck, it is a certainty, from the body language of this buck, that there definitely was another.

The photos on these two pages are selections from a photo sequence which I took during November, on a large ranch where I was working on whitetail photography. I had been trying to get some shots of a weird double-beamed non-typical buck, which I had finally located in a very large oat field. These two bucks, and a couple of others were also in the field, along with a half dozen does. The rut was in full swing, and one of the does was obviously in estrus or about to be. One of these bucks was jealously guarding her from the approaches of the other bucks. It seemed like he had them pretty well cowed down, when one of them decided to take him on. As soon as they started, they were into a completely crazed state of mind. The fight was extremely violent and non-stop. They were all over the large, dry oat field. Each was frantically lunging at the other, attempting to force him into a submissive position. They were both gasping for breath from the exertion, as well as from the mouthfuls of dry dirt. At one point during the frenzy, they pulled apart, and one made a headlong rush to broadside the other with his antlers. Just as the

antler tips hit the intended victim, he was able to side-step the blow. The first buck was so committed to the follow through, and had so much momentum, that he caught his antler tips in the dirt ...vaulting himself into a mid-air somersault. He hit the ground hard, landing on his back, but was immediately back up and fighting. After about eight or nine minutes of furious fighting, one of the bucks lost his footing and fell to the ground. The other buck began striking him violently, in the back, his sides and his belly. He was literally rolling the downed buck across the field. It appeared that he might very well kill him. Amazingly, the downed buck, desperate for his life, suddenly got to his feet and headed for the hills just as hard as he could run. The winner chased the loser for a short distance, then more or less escorted him out of the area. They were both exhausted and gasping for breath. In only one or two of my photos I found small amounts of blood on the antlers of the winner. I wouldn't be surprised if the loser sustained some serious injuries, but it is unknown. These were wild bucks, and I never saw either of them again.

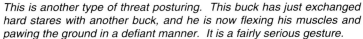

This is another type of threat posturing. This buck has just exchanged hard stares with another buck, and he is now flexing his muscles and pawing the ground in a defiant manner. It is a fairly serious gesture.

The buck on the left has broken the entire main beam off his right side. I found him in an area which had a very high buck popu-lation, with many mature bucks and a high buck-to-doe ratio. In such a situation (not a common one), there is a lot of fighting and by late fall or early winter many of the bucks will have broken antlers from fighting. It takes an incredible amount of force to break a main beam. Incidentally, this buck is not particularly old, probably 3½ years. He shows great antler potential.

More proof that some fights are deadly serious. The buck at the top left has been gored in the belly ...see how his gut is ballooning out. This is a very serious injury which might well kill him. However, I saw him again about two weeks later and he was beginning to heal. The buck on the bottom has apparently ripped his neck open while fighting and then it has become very irritated and infected. He reached up several times with his front hoof to paw at the wound. He was seen several times and apparently the infection lasted at least four to six weeks, but in the end he survived. I found him again at the same waterhole the next October, and he had a tremendous set of antlers with a big drop-tine ...and a scar on his neck. In the upper right corner are the skulls of two bucks which had locked their antlers while fighting. They were found in the spring by a turkey hunter.

These are selections from a photo sequence which was taken in December. As I watched from my deer blind, there were a number of deer, perhaps 20, in the feeding area in front of me. There were several bucks present, including a mature, heavy-bodied eight pointer with acorn points on some of his tines. He was strutting around like a peacock and displaying a considerable amount of "attitude." As the group fed in relative harmony, another large buck came out of the brushline a few hundred yards away, and started toward the other deer. I had seen this buck on two previous occasions. He was very mature, perhaps 7½ years old, and carried a wide rack with stickers and a major drop-tine. The drop-tine buck stopped about 30 yards short of the main concentration of deer and just stood there for several minutes, staring at the big eight-pointer most of the time. The eight-pointer slowly began walking towards the drop-tine buck. The closer he got, the more evident it became that there would be a confrontation. His ears went down, his

head was cocked and his eyes started bulging. His steps became stiff and slightly sideways. He made the hair stand up all over his body, which made him appear to be almost black. The drop-tine buck didn't back down. They walked parallel to each other for 15 or 20 seconds, perhaps sizing each other up. Then, the drop-tine buck abruptly stopped and turned directly at the other deer. He exploded into the eight-pointer, who came right back at him. It was a very serious knock-down, drag-out affair ...very noisy, with a tremendous amount of grunting and wheezing, along with a great deal of antler clatter. It was so loud that a hunter who was stationed in another blind at least a quarter mile away, clearly heard the fight. The two bucks were incredibly focused on each other. Looking back, I prob-ably could have come out of the blind and approached the two deer and they would not have cared. But I was too busy trying to get these photographs. It was a dark, overcast, late afternoon and much too dark for any action photography on color film. As soon as I realized what was about to happen, I rigged an extra cam-era with high-speed black and white film. I barely had it ready in time, and shot these pictures out the side of my blind. The fight lasted perhaps three minutes and the two bucks seemed to be pretty well matched up. As you can see, in the end, the eight-pointer ran the big drop-tine buck away. The drop-tine buck ran about 200 yards down the fenceline, then jumped over and disappeared into the brush. Within five minutes he trotted back out across a field, and jumped the fence to re-join the group of deer. He did however keep his distance from the eight-pointer after that.

Where social communications are concerned, the whitetail's use of personal odors and sense of smell could hardly be overrated. From the glands on the forehead to the inter-digital glands between the toes, whitetails depend heavily upon the use of personal scents in communicating identities, territories and status to other deer. Their "scent" vocabulary is amazing.

WHITETAIL COMMUNICATION

This incredibly tall-tined buck is performing the flehmen behavior, concentrating the available odors in his mouth, actually "tasting" the scents. Bucks commonly do this, particularly when they come to a spot where a doe has urinated. They will taste the grass and ground which contains the odor and then raise their head back, savoring the odors. It primes reproductive readiness.

Whitetails are great communicators. When you consider that the vast majority of their communications are carried out silently, with posturing and sight, and through the dispersion and interpretation of scent, their success in this area is even more remarkable.

We've already covered a great deal of whitetail communication techniques in discussing the "dominance factor" and its related social behaviors. Most of these methods of communicating are driven by aggressive tendencies. They are the build-

ing blocks which define the social structure of any given group of whitetails. There are a number of additional, commonly observed ways that whitetails communicate. Beyond the aggressive-type communications, the two most obvious categories would be "sexual" communications and "warning" communications.

Needless to say the majority of sexual communications are tied in with the "rut." At that time of the year, procreation and the perpetuation of the species becomes all encompassing in the world of the whitetail. Where sexual communications and the rut

The famous "buck rubs" made by whitetails serve a variety of different purposes. This activity functions as a workout, strengthening neck muscles and improving coordination. Rubs also function as "signposts," visible markers staking out a buck's domain. Further, they also act as repositories for scent deposited from the forehead and orally ...scents which serve as communicators.

Rubs are not always made on vertical trees, as you can see. This deep-woods buck is marking a small fallen tree. He rubbed it with his forehead and then licked it thoroughly.

are concerned, almost all communications are carried out through the use of scents. With their highly developed sense of smell, whitetails are able to differentiate odors in ways that we can only imagine. In fact it's hard to even imagine what they can accomplish in this way. Through the use and interpretation of personal scents, whitetails are able to advertise (or determine) sex, identity, status, presence and territorial delineation. That's a lot of information.

During the pre-rut period, after bucks have removed the velvet from their newly grown antlers, they begin to make "rubs" on saplings and trees. Part of this activity is borne out of their increased aggressiveness. Due to hormonal changes, they are becoming increasingly belligerent. They seem to literally take out some of their frustrations on the vegetation around them. These rubbing routines are performed frequently, and are sometimes

Rubs can be utilized to some extent in determining the travel patterns of whitetails. Bucks tend to travel the same approximate routes and many of the rubs are used over and over ...not only by the one buck who initiated it, but in some cases by a number of different animals. This buck did not rub the tree, but he did approach it directly to smell the trunk. Perhaps a more dominant animal had left his scent, which caused this buck to back off and look around apprehensively in case the other buck was present.

quite lengthy. Occasionally a buck may work on a rub for 10, 20, even 30 minutes at a time. This actually functions as a physical workout for the buck, helping to strengthen and build up his neck muscles, and improving his overall coordination. One of the most remarkable physical transformations that a whitetail buck goes

The making of "scrapes", or "scraping," is a major communication tool used primarily in relation to the rut. An area of ground is scraped clean, by pawing with the hoof, and urine is deposited in the fresh dirt. There is usually, but not always, an overhanging branch, which is mouthed, chewed and rubbed with the forehead, leaving scents that delineate status, identity and territory.

Signpost "rubs" also occasionally function as "scrapes". I've observed a considerable number of situations when a buck approached a rub, smelled and rubbed it, then scraped.

through during the rut is the increase in the size of his neck muscles. This varies tremendously among individuals, no doubt based on many factors such as age, size, health and status. The necks of some bucks become so much larger in the fall, that it may almost render them unrecognizable from their late-summer selves. It is amazing that muscle mass can be built up to that degree in such a relatively short period. Some bucks which may have a "summer" neck circumference of 14 to 18 inches, may have a neck size of as much as 30 inches or more only three months later! The big-necked bucks are frequently the more dominant animals who are in their

Generally speaking, more scraping activity is carried out by older bucks than by younger deer. A variety of different deer may utilize a scrape once it has been initiated, repeatedly re-visiting and "freshening" it. The idea apparently is to cover up all previous deer scents with their own, and be sure that should a sexually interested doe visit the scrape, that their scent will predominate.

prime. They have worked themselves (and their muscles) into a frenzy, sometimes making huge numbers of rubs and frequently mock-fighting with bushes and shrubs. Their necks occasionally become freakish and grotesque.

Beyond the "aggressive" drive to make rubs and work out frustrations, the rubs are also used in other ways. Most times, rubs are made on trees in a fashion where the rub is a highly visible marker. This possibly delineates territory, and at the least, it advertises a buck's presence. Further, scent is prodigiously applied to the rub by rubbing the forehead glands, and by licking and mouthing the tree.

Usually, the first thing a buck will do when approaching a rub will be to carefully sniff the rub for the information it contains. Then, he will likely begin to cover up and replace that information with scent information of his own. Some of the major

This buck, who is standing near a doe apparently coming into estrus, has thoroughly rubbed the overhead branch with his forehead and is vigorously mouthing and tasting the branch.

There were several does and a couple of other bucks in sight when this mature buck approached the area. As he reached up to hook the branches of a tree (perhaps to impress the other deer), one of the limbs was dead and broke off, a portion of it falling on the buck's head and lodging in his antlers. He actually seemed rather pleased with himself and performed the flehmen behavior.

signpost rubs which are used frequently by a variety of different bucks must be like those bulletin boards you see in front of supermarkets, where the letters and the messages are constantly being changed. The more aggressive, dominant, and active bucks do a lot of rubbing in an apparent effort to be sure that their advertising messages are the most prevalent and the most recent, in as many places as possible.

Another activity which begins later, but which parallels rubbing activity to some extent, is the making of "scrapes." Used primarily in relation to the rut, scrapes are a major communication tool where breeding is concerned. An area of ground is scraped clean by pawing with the front hooves, and urine is deposited in the fresh dirt. Sometimes the buck will perform a "rub-urination" behavior in which he rubs the metatarsal glands on his hind legs together as he lets the urine wash over them to the ground. Assumedly this behavior enhances the dispersal of scents advertising his sexual status to does in the area. These scents may also act as an intimidating factor toward other lesser bucks or would-be competitors.

Where scrapes are located, there is usually, but not always, an overhanging branch from a tree. An important part of the scraping ritual is the mouthing, chewing and forehead-rubbing of the overhanging branch. Apparently the scents disperse more efficiently from the branch, which is hanging in mid-air above ground level.

More times than not, the branch is just high enough over the scrape that a buck has to stretch his neck a little to reach it and work it over. Sometimes a buck will have to stand erect on his hind legs and stretch his neck just to reach it.

Once, on a cold November morning as I watched a large mature buck make his way along a brushy creek, he stopped and began pawing a scrape. I was watching through some brush, but there didn't seem to be any overhanging branches. However as he completed his "freshening" on the ground portion of the scrape, he not only stood up high on his hind legs, but had to hop up and down repeatedly to be able to touch and lick the overhanging branch, or "licking branch" as it's commonly called.

A great deal of importance seems to be attached to these scent "billboards." During the heat of the rut, they seem to draw deer like a magnet. Much the same as with rubs, the more active and dominant bucks re-visit and freshen the scrapes frequently. They work feverishly to cover up all previous buck scents with their own, to be sure that, should a sexually interested doe visit the scrape, their scent will predominate. Bucks of all ages work scrapes, but it seems that the older, more mature bucks are much more serious about it.

Another commonly observed behavior which involves perhaps another level of odor communication is called the "flehmen" behavior. Among hunters and observers, it is more commonly called a "lip-curl." In performing a lip-curl, a buck aims his nose slightly up, opens his mouth slightly, and curls his top lip up and back severely, flattening his nose somewhat. Bucks commonly perform this behavior, particularly when they come to a spot where a doe has urinated. They will taste the grass

The depositing of scent on the overhead branch which usually accompanies a scrape, acts like an advertising billboard. Other deer that pass nearby will be drawn to it like a magnet.

As the rut approaches, the various doe-groups are visited more and more frequently by bucks trying to find a sexual partner. Pheromones which are released by a doe's body contain signals as to the doe's sexual status. As her estrous state approaches, the pheromones act as a stimulant to the buck's already libidinous sexual state.

I zeroed in on this 12-pointer because it was such a clean crisp shot of the flehmen behavior. He was actually standing in the middle of a doe group. He had just arrived at the site.

and ground which contains the odor and raise their head back, savoring it.

In the past, many people commonly thought that this behavior told the buck whether or not a particular doe was in estrus. It actually functions as a sexual stimulant. There is a special organ in the roof of the mouth that utilizes this scent information to maintain and prime the buck's sexual libido. Obviously, some sexual scent information is carried by the urine, but lip-curling is sometimes performed without the tasting of urine at all — with the stimulant or pheromone apparently airborne. Many times, a buck will perform a lip-curl when no other deer are currently present, but it seems that the behavior is more frequent and more pronounced when bucks are in the company of a doe or doe-group. This behavior is performed by bucks of all ages.

The universe of sexual communications among whitetails is a complex one, and there is much that is not fully understood. Whitetail interaction in this area is fascinating to watch, but somewhat difficult, since much breeding activity seems to be done nocturnally. After all of the rubbing and scraping rituals, the bucks eventually do get together with does which are coming into estrus. Even then, there is more ritual behavior. Typically a buck (or more likely several bucks) will locate a doe, a day or two before she actually comes into estrus. Then, the buck (or the most dominant buck) will more or less "stand guard" over the doe until the time when she is ready to accept him. Many times she will act nonchalant and uninterested during this period, but he will stand alert, many times within 10 yards, and charge any other buck (or any other animal) which threatens to come near. Finally, as her time approaches, she forces him to play a cat-and-mouse game in which she coyly runs away and he has to catch her. Just as he almost has her, she takes off again. Sometimes this seems to go on forever, but eventually she submits, and the short breeding process is consummated.

I should mention here that during the courting process, there is one additional form of communication that frequently takes place. Verbal communication by the buck is the now well known "buck grunt." Many times, while either on the trail of a doe in estrus, or while actually with a doe, a buck emits a series of low, short, pig-like grunts. The series may consist of only one grunt, or it may consist of as many as five or six consecutive grunts with short intervals in between. I don't believe the full significance of these grunts is completely understood. They seem to be closely

What a set of brow-tines! This is a very mature buck performing flehmen, but actually, bucks of all ages perform this behavior. He' has just stepped out of the shadows on a fall morning. As is so commonly the case, there were a couple of does nearby.

The young doe in this photo was obviously in estrus, or just about to be. The wide-racked nine-pointer in the background was herding her like a sheep dog, not letting her out of his sight as he postured and threatened another less dominant buck.

While it's not readily visible in the photo, there's a thin layer of frost on this buck's antlers, on a cold November morning. At the time of this photo, I could actually hear him "grunting" as he followed close behind a doe. Within the next few minutes he bred the doe about 100 yards away from my blind.

tied in with a "near-breeding" situation. I've heard bucks grunt many times but I've never heard a doe grunt during these sexual encounters. Callers have been using the technique of "grunting" up bucks for some time, with varying degrees of success. Personally, I've had much better overall results simply by rattling antlers but I have also had considerable success using nothing more than a grunt call.

Yet another group of communication techniques used by whitetails would be the "warning" communications. For once, these have nothing to do with dominance or aggression, and nothing to do with sex. One of the most common behaviors to be observed by anyone who has watched whitetails much, is tail-flaring, or "flagging." When a whitetail senses danger, or feels uncertainty, or fear, the tail is raised and flared, exhibiting the bright white underside. This is a highly visible warning, and usually all other deer in the vicinity will take heed immediately. It's an effective, efficient warning device. It also helps deer in a group to visually stay together as they flee.

There is yet another interesting function of the whitetail's name-sake appendage. Whitetail fawns key in on their mothers' white tails in order to follow them, at least to some extent. It has been demonstrated that if a man runs through the woods waving a white handkerchief — in sight of a whitetail fawn — the fawn will instinctively follow the waving white "flag."

If you've encountered white-tails in the woods at all, then

I watched this pair go through the mating rituals twice, as I slipped up on them in the woods on a cold, rainy November morning. There was a second subordinate buck who kept running in but he was no match for this buck.

With a scene unfolding like this one, breeding could take place at almost any moment. The time was the peak of the rut and this big, very mature buck was guarding the doe very closely. There were two or three other bucks on the sidelines, who were wishing they were in his position, but every time one of them even thought about coming closer, this buck put on a very dominant posturing show. They were obviously afraid of him. Her posture seems to indicate that she might submit to him at almost any time.

Tail-flaring or "flagging" is a common means of communication used by whitetails. It's an expression of fear and a warning. The white flag is highly visible and other deer usually take heed immediately. If there is a group of deer present, the raising of one "flag" normally sends them ALL into flight.

you're sure to be familiar with the white-tail's most common verbal signal, the "blow," or "snort." One of the most common experiences in the deer woods is hearing a deer "blowing" or "snorting" as it runs away from you. Many times you'll hear the alarm signal, but never lay eyes on the deer that made it.

Another expression of apprehension, which is also used as a warning, is the foot-stomp. Many times, when deer feel uncertain or afraid, they will stomp the ground repeatedly, keeping a close watch on that which has startled them. I've also watched whitetails use the foot-stomp in a seemingly different context. This probably should come under the heading of "intelligence" rather than "communication." Many times I've watched whitetails, as they became somewhat startled, or uncertain about a motionless object (me, in many cases). They'll tense up, every muscle on full alert, and stare intently at the object, looking for the slightest movement.

They suspect the object may present a possible danger but they're not sure. If the object doesn't move, they will begin stomping the ground, trying to startle the object into moving, and perhaps to alert the other deer. If the object still doesn't move, the deer may lower its head to the ground, pretending to eat and ignore the object, but then will jerk the head back up to see if the object was fooled and has moved. I've seen a deer go through this whole routine repeatedly, as many as a dozen times, standing in one spot. It's just another fascinating behavior that whitetails perform.

One other type of warning communication which is quite incredible, and which has been observed a number of times, is a

When you have a whitetail reacting toward you in this manner, you've been discovered ...no matter how well hidden you thought you were. She may bob her head and stomp and wave her flag first, but chances are she'll be gone soon.

Another expression of apprehension, which is also used as a warning is the foot-stomp. Many times, when deer feel uncertain or afraid, they will stomp the ground repeatedly, keeping a close watch on that which has startled them. This old warrior has been startled by the noise from my camera. He's an interesting old deer, with massive antlers. His eyes are red and his bottom lip is ripped from fighting. For some reason his testicles are greatly enlarged.

warning communicated by scent. When a whitetail has been startled or frightened, and has fled, an expression of this fear, in the form of a scent, is left behind. Another deer may arrive at the same spot, perhaps by chance, after a short time has passed. Frequently, as the new deer reaches the spot at which the previous deer became frightened, the "new" deer will react with fear and flee also, even though the danger may no longer be present.

In summary, whitetails are terrific communicators, very efficient with a multitude of postures, and an almost unbelievable ability to send and receive scent messages. To a very large extent, whitetails live by their nose. The communication devices which carry out their social rituals are complex and not fully understood. The more you observe and study, the more interesting nuances and characteristics you find.

THE MAGIC OF ANTLERS

I suspect that antlers have fascinated mankind ever since some early human saw them for the first time. Early peoples admired them, collected them, used them for tools and decoration and considered them valuable. Modern man is no different. The monster buck pictured above fairly well epitomizes whitetail antlers. He carries the majority of the most admired attributes ...massive weight, tall tines, long beams, attractive overall symmetry, interesting character and 20 points over one inch long.

While whitetail bucks are certainly very individual in many respects, the one thing that truly makes each of them different and completely unique is their crowning glory — their antlers. No two sets are exactly alike, much like fingerprints. The diversity of antler sizes and shapes is practically limitless. Not only is there tremendous diversity from animal to animal, there are also differences from year to year for each individual animal. For whitetail hunters and enthusiasts, each year is a whole new world where antlers are concerned. Not only will you find new bucks which you've never seen before, you'll also find previously seen bucks with new and perhaps significantly different antlers. It's a very exciting phenomenon.

Man seems to have always been fascinated by these magical head-bones, probably ever since some ancient, hairy-backed hominid came upon his first whitetail buck. However it began, people of early

You can see the "velvet" texture on this young buck's antlers. The velvety skin covers a mass of blood vessels feeding the rapidly growing antlers. If you were able to touch a live buck's growing velvet antlers, they would be mostly soft and very warm to the touch.

After a whitetail buck has shed his old antlers, the new antlers begin to form and grow almost immediately. At first, the new growth seems to be very slow getting started, but then it gains speed like a runaway train, growing to completion in only 100 to 120 days. This buck was photographed in late April, possibly six to eight weeks after shedding.

cultures long ago came to admire antlers. They collected them and used some for tools and decorations. Others were used in social rituals. Special antlers have long been sought as status symbols, and they've been considered valuable for thousands of years. Man's feelings toward whitetail antlers are much the same today as they've always been.

As mentioned, whitetail antlers come in almost every conceivable size and shape. This in itself creates a broad base of interest for collector-minded humans. However, they are perhaps even more awe-inspiring in their ability to change form and appear and disappear, through a somewhat mystical sequence of events. A buck begins the spring with virtually no antlers, and then they appear as if by magic over the short period of summer. All at once, at the end of summer, their appearance is dramatically transformed. Then, during winter, they suddenly disappear again.

Some antlers appear graceful, slender, and fragile, yet they're almost impossible to break. Others are grotesque, almost other-worldly.

These three photos of the same buck were taken over a six-week period. The photo on the left was taken on June 15, the middle photo was taken on July 10, and the third photo was taken on August 1. Notice in the last picture how the tips of the tines are bulbous and shiny. This indicates that they are still growing. Even though they will grow some more, the rack is probably 90% complete in terms of size. After full size is attained, the velvet remains for another four to six weeks while the antlers harden fully.

At times they have a velvet fur growing on them, they're occasionally covered with blood, and at other times they're shiny and polished, with colors ranging from creamy white to almost black. The mysterious and diverse nature of whitetail antlers is such a curious phenomenon, that nothing else compares.

To begin with, "antlers" are very different from "horns," even though the two terms are sometimes used interchangeably on a colloquial basis. Antlers, which are grown only by the deer family

This photo, taken about the first of July, shows a nicely developing 10-point rack. This buck and I surprised each other as I drove through a ranch late one morning. I made a quick stop and took this shot as he stood in the tall weeds.

When you're traveling through whitetail country, you just never know what sights await you. This was an impressive mid-August sight, if I ever saw one. The buck in the rear is a 6x7 typical, and the one in the front is a 5x5 typical. Both are large deer, and standing in this position, they appear to have been cut from the same mold. They may very well share the same bloodlines.

This buck shows the results of a few months of easy living ...a beautiful, smooth summer coat, changing to winter-gray, a fat belly and a most impressive new set of monstrous antlers. Summer can be a hard time on whitetails, depending on the weather. This was a lucky year for this whitetail, as the temperatures had been mild, with plenty of rain.

I photographed this buck with massive antlers one morning as he foraged his way through the heavy green weeds. The time was September and his velvet would be coming off any time now. He has several interesting characteristics, including several non-typical points and matching drop-tines off the lower part of each beam. However, his extreme mass is probably his most impressive quality.

(and only by males, with the exception of caribou), consist of solid bone and are shed and regrown each year. Horns, on the other hand, which are grown by cattle, goats, sheep, and some other hooved animals, consist of a permanent bony core covered by a keratin sheath. Horns are generally not shed and re-grown.

Annual cycles of whitetail antler growth are stimulated and controlled by the level of the male hormone, testosterone. The testosterone level is controlled by the pituitary gland, which in turn is influenced by the photoperiod, or day-length.

Each year, throughout the majority of the whitetail's range, most whitetail bucks shed or cast off their antlers in January, February, or March, depending on the specific area and the health of the individual. The antlers literally fall off their heads, usually with nothing more than the force of gravity to assist them. Sometimes they are shed simultaneously, and other times they are dropped many days apart. Occasionally they are dropped within sight of each other, but more frequently they're dropped at different locations, anywhere from a hundred yards apart to perhaps a mile or more. As obvious as it seems these "sheds" would be, it can be surprisingly difficult to search out and find shed antlers after they've been cast off. Further, finding a matched pair in the wild is a challenge which is rarely met. It's true that many disappear because they are consumed by rodents and other animals, but the larger fact is that they are simply hard to see. They tend to blend into the other debris of the deer woods incredibly well.

After the bucks have shed their antlers, they are left with nothing but two bloody pedicles on their heads. The pedicles are bony outgrowths from the skull which are the origination points, or staging areas, from which new antlers will grow. The bleeding is brief and inconsequential and the pedicles quickly heal over the next few days. The genetic information, with the "blueprints" for the next set of antlers is

In this photo, taken in late August, the blood supply has been cut off from the antlers, and the velvet has begun to shrink and crack. The velvet will probably be removed soon.

Here is visual proof that the exact timing for the removal of velvet is a very individual matter. This photo was taken about the first of September. The big buck on the left, with the weirdly-shaped tall antlers is still in full velvet. The little yearling buck in the foreground has already removed all his velvet. The huge buck coming up in the rear, is in the process of removing his velvet .

It's the end of summer and these two big mature 10-pointers are still summer pals, but not for long. The heavy-antlered buck in the rear appears to have just begun taking the velvet from his antlers, as evidenced by the blood. There is an outside possibility that he has been sparring with some other buck and bloodied his antlers in that way. It would be unusual at this stage, but not unheard of.

Here is a two-buck bachelor group in September. One buck has shed his velvet completely, perhaps several days before, while the other hasn't even started yet.

activated, and the re-growth of new antlers is set into motion almost immediately. A swelling bud begins to form on each pedicle after a few weeks. By mid-April, over most of the whitetail's range, the new antlers begin to grow. The new antlers are covered with a soft, hairy skin containing numerous blood vessels, which supply the rapidly growing antlers with nourishment. This specialized skin has a fuzzy appearance and has come to be called "velvet."

As spring progresses and the bucks try to recoup from the stress and damage of fall and winter, the antlers slowly begin to grow. Actually, antlers are said to be the fastest growing bones in the world and I've no doubt that they are. However, at this early stage of development, the apparent progress is very slow compared to the rate of growth later in the summer. Much of a buck's nutritional intake, as well as his nutritional reserves, if any, are directed to the growth of his new antlers. He needs all the nutritional intake he can get, and this time period is primarily characterized by eating, drinking and resting.

Spring is of course followed by summer, which brings on raging torrents of growth in whitetail antlers. Then, it becomes easy to see why they're considered to be the world's fastest growing bones, as they gain speed like a runaway train. I've heard estimates of growth rates anywhere from an inch per week to an inch per day. Reality may lie somewhere in between these two. I don't know what the scientific answer is, if any, but the growth rate is phenomenal. If you were to see a given buck in mid-summer, and then see him again two or three weeks later, you'd surely be impressed. It's one of the most wondrous acts of nature, certainly worthy of its "magical" status. The antlers grow from their tips, with the shiny, bulbous, swollen tips indicative of rapid growth.

The majority of the visible growth is accomplished in June, July, and early August in most areas. For all intents and purposes, the new antlers have attained their total magnitude in 100 to 120 days. By late summer they are essentially full-grown. The buck will wear the velvet for another four to six weeks as the antlers mature and completely harden. Generally, by sometime in August, it's possible to determine just how large a rack will be and how many points it will have. The big racks look monstrous in August.

Depending upon the precise geographic location and individual characteristics, a major change takes

These two bucks were photographed at different times and places, but they both show the process of velvet removal. The buck at the top appears to have shed his velvet perhaps a day or two previously, but for some reason he hasn't bothered to complete the process. The buck in the lower photo has just shredded his velvet in the last hour.

So-called "typical" antlers are formed in such a way that all of the tines are upright and more or less in-line on the top of the beams. Perhaps the most common conformation in the world, on a buck with any maturity, is a "typical" eight-point rack. Towards the other extreme, a buck such as the one pictured above, with a 6x7 typical frame, is a very rare animal.

Here is another 6x7 "typical" antler mainframe. On this buck, there is a small extra point on the first tall tine of each side, making him a 15-pointer.

place in the late-August to early-October time frame. As day-length shortens, new hormonal instructions are sent to the pedicles and the newly grown antlers. The blood flow is reduced and then cut off at the pedicles, and the velvet begins to shrink and dry. The antler tips are no longer bulbous and shiny. The new antlers complete the process of hardening as minerals are deposited in the final stages of nutrient transmission. The velvet may begin to crack and split after the antlers have hardened completely.

Then, prompted by a silent signal from within, whitetail bucks proceed to remove the velvet by rubbing their antlers on trees, shrubs, fence posts, or anything else that's handy. Generally speaking, the task is not too difficult, as the velvet practically falls off of its own accord much of the time. Depending on how much the velvet has dried out, there is sometimes a good deal

The buck pictured here just barely makes it into an extremely rare category. The last small one-inch points on each beam make him a perfect 7x7, 14-point typical. He has beautiful symmetry, and good antler-mass. While he's certainly no youngster, he doesn't appear fully mature. There's a chance he may become even better in future years. Honest 7x7s are extremely rare.

Here is another big typical-antlered buck. His mainframe consists of six typical points on each side and he has a couple of extra "kicker" points. Even 12-point typical antlers are quite rare, when the overall universe of whitetail antlers is considered. Most 12-point racks are actually 8, 9, 10 or 11 point mainframes, with non-typical points making up the difference.

Yet another 6x7 typical buck. Interestingly, I photographed this buck within 500 yards of the spot where I photographed the 6x7 at the top of page 94, but five years later. Genetics?

of blood on the antlers and face, while at other times there is little or none. The entire process of velvet removal is usually carried out in a relatively short time, perhaps only an hour or two. In short order, the soft, fuzzy "summer" look is replaced with hard, shiny, new "fall" antlers.

Whitetail antlers vary tremendously in their coloration. It seems to be quite an individual matter, but the primary influence on coloration is the blood from the velvet. The color may actually vary somewhat depending on how dried-out the velvet is at the time of removal. The color of antlers is also influenced, but to a lesser extent, by the types of vegetation that the new antlers are rubbed on.

Once the new antlers are completely grown, hardened and polished, they'll function as status symbols, rubbing instru-

The buck above is a huge 10-point typical. Ten-point typicals are common, but not of this magnitude. The old buck on the right could be called a 7x7 typical, if you gave him credit for the stub of his last point, broken off on his left side. I call him old, because I had seen him, off and on for four or five years ...and he was a big, mature 6x6 12-pointer the first time I ever saw him.

ments, weapons and quite possibly as sexual attractants. A mature buck seems to wear his crown as though it were a badge of honor. Big bucks tend to stand with a regal bearing, holding their antlers high for all to see. Bucks of all sizes seem to be very aware of antler size, both theirs and others. Bucks with large antlers seem to be aware of the exact size and proportion of all their points, and are able to maneuver them very precisely through all manner of tight spaces — even during high-speed travel in heavy cover.

97

You can't see all the points on these freakish antlers. You'll just have to trust me. There are at least 22 substantial points, including three drop-tines, and three beams on the right side. There are head-bones going in all directions.

This is a really strange set of non-typical antlers, with double upright beams. The fog was so thick, I could barely see through it. The mystical mood was almost other-worldly.

The antlers serve their purposes well, throughout the fall and early winter, rubbing trees, impressing other bucks, fighting fights and hopefully attracting the prettiest does around. As the rut winds down, the testosterone level decreases. The antlers are no longer needed and the cycle is completed. They are cast and fall to the ground, just like all antlers before them.

It's a magical cycle, pretty impressive on all counts. However, if you're really a hard case, and the cycle itself doesn't impress you, then surely some of the antlers produced by the cycle will. Whitetail antlers are some of nature's most creative work.

While it is unknown whether or not primitive hunters counted the number of points or measured the widths of antlers, they surely must have noticed when they took an animal with particularly large or interesting antlers. Just as modern man has improved his communication levels in

For connoisseurs of non-typical whitetail antlers, this is a beautiful sight. His antlers are wide and heavy, but the three big heavy drop-tines overshadow the rest. Whitetails with one or two drop-tines are quite rare, in fact most people are not likely to ever see one. Needless to say, a triple drop-tine buck is extremely rare.

This interesting south Texas non-typical buck, photographed in the wild, has 18 good points. His antlers are very massive, but perhaps his most outstanding characteristic is his brow tines which are heavy, multi-pointed, and about 10 inches long. His typical mainframe is a 5x6, with seven non-typical points in the form of forks and kickers. I hunted this buck with my camera for two weeks to get this photo.

This non-typical buck has short points, but he's enormous overall ...extremely wide and massive. He has seven points on his left side and 14 points on his right, 21 points total.

other aspects of life, we've also improved our communication levels regarding whitetail antlers. As we've studied and admired them, we've classified and categorized them in a number of ways.

One of the most basic classifications is the determination as to whether a set of antlers would be considered "typical" or "non-typical." "Typical" antlers are easily the more common, and are generally thought of as an in-line series of smooth vertical points (or tines) coming off a more or less horizontal, forward-sweeping main beam. The overwhelming majority of whitetail bucks which are 2½ years old or more, grow antlers which are essentially typical in form. To take it a step further, it appears that the vast majority of bucks in most areas grow essentially typical "eight-point" antlers, with four points on each side. I've observed literally thousands and thousands of different bucks and I would

To see a world-class non-typical buck like this, in a split-second opportunity, will definitely make the hair on your neck stand up. He carries 18 points ...a massive 5x5 mainframe, plus two major forks and six big sticker points. You've gotta love him. Note the small bloody patch on the lower part of his neck. He had apparently been fighting.

estimate that "basic" eight-point bucks make up somewhere in the range of 60% to 80% of the "2½ years or older" buck populations which I observe. While there are many typical-framed bucks out there with 6, 7, 9, 10, 11, or more typical points, they aren't nearly as numerous as the ubiquitous eight-pointers.

"Non-typical" antlers, while not nearly as common as typicals, get a broadly disproportionate share of attention. Non-typical antlers are usually thought of as having or being made up of weird or abnormal points. The base frame may be more or less typical in shape, but the "freak," or "abnormal," or "weird" points may be present in almost any fashion. The extra points come in all kinds of shapes and sizes and may stick out in just about any

Another interesting non-typical. This buck's forte is height and mass. He carries a 5x5 typical mainframe, and has at least nine additional sticker points, for 19 points total.

This nice double drop-tine buck has 17 points. I had seen this buck in each of the two previous years, once from this same blind, and once from another blind not too far away. Two years before, he had a substantial 5x6 mainframe with one sticker point but no drop-tines. The year before, he had a massive 5x6 typical frame, with one big drop-tine on his right side. Drop-tines appear unpredictably and they may or may not repeat from year to year. This buck wasn't seen on the ranch for almost a year after this photo was taken. Then his remains were found by a hunter. His antlers were locked with those of another buck, who had also perished in the fight.

If you're one of those people who want it all ...here it is. I didn't get to see this buck nearly as long or as closely as I would have liked, but I feel fortunate that I saw him at all. He has a giant 6x6 typical mainframe, with deep forks and big sticker points everywhere. One sticker point is 9 or 10 inches long. With at least 21 points, wide, heavy, tall, super-long beams ...he's got it all.

direction. These points go by many names and descriptions, according to their shape, size and location on the rack. Depending on who's giving the description, or what part of the country you're in, you may hear terms like "stickers," "cheaters," "kickers," "drop-tines," "forked-tines," "double-drops," "webbed points," "double-brows," "double-beams" or simply "extra points." For most whitetail nuts, the more of all these things, the better.

I don't know about primitive man, but for modern man, whitetails with big non-typical antlers have always demanded the use of lots of adjectives and exclamation points. On those rare occasions when a hunter gets to see an interesting non-typical buck, he's not very likely to be calm about the experience. They are very exciting animals, and very rare. The lucky

Non-typicals aren't always monstrous, as this photo shows. He's a tiny little buck, 2½ years old at the most, and he has double drop-tines. It's unusual for deer this young to have major non-typical characteristics. I never saw him again.

This is an impressive buck ...fully mature, heavy-bodied, a 5x6 typical mainframe and a substantial drop-tine. As I watched him and several other deer from my deer blind, it seemed obvious that he was the lord and master of that area ...at least for the time being.

hunter or observer is likely to rant, and rave and carry on about it like a madman.

Many hunting areas around the country have a cherished legendary buck. This is either a giant which was taken in years past, or an unbelievable buck which has been seen, but which repeatedly eludes the local experts. Many such bucks are factual, and documented but some seem to be more magical than actual. In either event, it would seem that the majority of "legendary" bucks turn out to be non-typicals. Big non-typicals are never forgotten.

To one way of thinking, the non-typical concept extends beyond simply weird points. After all, at least part of the non-typical mystique is based on its rarity. In fact, a whitetail with substantial non-typical characteristics is a truly rare item and very much "out of the ordinary." Non-typical could be thought of as "non-ordinary."

Another type of antlers also is very much "out of the ordinary." There are several "typical" characteristics, that when observed in their extremes, are also very rare. While double-drop-tine bucks are so rare that the vast majority of hunters could search for a lifetime without ever even seeing one, the same could be said for 7x7 typical bucks. They exist, just as double-drops do, but don't necessarily count on seeing one in this lifetime. Even 6x6 "all typical" bucks are quite rare, when compared to the rest of the whitetail population. The vast majority of twelve-point bucks have 8, 9, 10 or 11-point mainframes with additional non-typical points making up the difference.

The point is, that for some purposes, extreme "typical" characteristics can be just as "non-typical" or "non-ordinary" as freak points, and as such might be thought of in the same vein. I suspect that a typical buck with 15-inch tines might affect most people much the same way that a buck with a drop-tine would. They're both about equally "out of the ordinary," and either would be considered an exciting rarity.

Undoubtedly, we could define, classify, and qualify antler terms and characteristics almost indefinitely. The overriding factor remains that most whitetail enthusiasts are fascinated by antlers. Big, weird antlers hold a special appeal for many — the bigger and weirder, the better.

One of the great things about whitetail antlers is that, no matter how many you've

This buck, even though he is extremely narrow, has such incredible mass and height that he would score enough to make the Boone and Crockett record book.

This old buck had been seen on and off for many years. He had almost always been a smooth typical 10-pointer, until this year. He'd been injured in a fight the year before.

seen, no matter how big or how strange, there is always another set out there somewhere which is bigger, or stranger, or more interesting. The fascination with whitetail antlers is perpetual.

The high level of interest in antler development in general, and non-typical antlers in particular, has permeated the ranks of all types of whitetail enthusiasts — hunters, ranchers, wildlife biologists, scientists and nature lovers. Considerable amounts of study and research have been done in trying to understand this phenomenon. Much has been learned, but it would seem that there are still many more questions than there are answers. In understanding the underlying causes for the growth of either typical or non-typical antlers, there are a number of factors to be

Many people get carried away by the spread, or width of a set of antlers. The antlers on this large-bodied buck are approaching the outer limits where spread is concerned. While wider bucks have been known, and taken by hunters, there probably haven't been too many of them. This buck's antler spread is estimated to be approximately 28 to 29 inches inside and 34 to 35 inches outside.

considered, including genetics, nutrition, age and even current or previous injuries. All of these, and probably other more subtle ingredients, go into the non-typical recipe. The question is, how much of each ingredient goes into the mix, in what sequence, and in what proportions, etc.

Genetics obviously play an important role in antler development. The apparent "passing on" of antler characteristics has been observed numerous times in a wide variety of diverse locations. Many localized areas are known to have a tendency to produce certain types of characteristics, for example; bifurcated (forked) tines, double brow tines, a tendency towards wide spreads, even drop-tines. Other areas show an almost complete absence of such characteristics. Even so, genetics is far from being the complete answer.

In these same regions, the extent of these characteristics may vary according to nutritional factors, age structure, and many other factors. Also, for many years, genetic potential was generally thought of as being passed down from older bucks to younger bucks. Only more recently has serious consideration been given to the fact that a buck's antler potential, via genetics, is derived from both parents. Recent research has even raised the possibility that genetic antler potential may be derived more from the mother than from the father.

Nutrition is certainly important, for both the general health and the antler growth of a whitetail buck. Chances are that you've read or heard that nutrition goes first toward the development of a buck's body. Then nutrition fosters antler growth after bodily needs are satisfied. While it's true to a point, it is also a bit of an oversimplification. The issue is a complex one. Even skinny, young, and malnourished bucks DO grow antlers, even if those antlers are rarely very impressive.

Nevertheless, before a buck can realize his genetic antler potential, or the potential to grow antlers based on his age, he must have adequate nutrition. It sounds fairly simple, but there's a little more to it than that. Just because a buck has an adequate,

Here are two examples of extraordinarily wide-racked bucks. The 12-point buck at the top has an estimated spread of about 26 inches inside the beams. The wide nine-pointer below is also somewhere in the range of 25 to 26 inches. A buck with a super-wide spread oftentimes makes a more dramatic first impression than another more narrow buck which may actually be much more substantial overall.

This buck is starving to death due to a lack of nutritional availability. He still grew antlers which would be considered pretty impressive in some places but just imagine what he might have grown with adequate nutrition.

Here is an example of a buck which is fully mature and in excellent health. He simply does not have the genetics to grow exceptionally large antlers. He was a dominant buck with a bad attitude and small antlers.

or even excessive amount of nutrition THIS YEAR does not necessarily mean that he will realize his antler potential THIS YEAR — even if he has great genetics and is fully mature. Recent studies and observations seem to indicate that, in order for a buck to grow to his maximum antler potential, a lot of things need to go right during his <u>entire</u> life cycle. This is especially true if a buck is to become a giant or "super-buck."

It probably helps if he was born early in a wet year, to a healthy, robust mother. This, and a first summer of mild conditions and plenty of food, will get him off to a running start. Some wildlife managers believe that it is important that the first THREE YEARS of his life be during a time of plenty, if he is to have a chance of growing to "super-buck" status. There is a possibility that if even one of the first four or five years of his life is a severe-drought year, with a lack of nutritional availability, that he may never recover to his FULL potential. It's very important that a whitetail buck maintain an adequate nutritional level on a constant year-round, year-to-year basis, if he is to live up to his potential. A large set of antlers, based on nutrition, is dependent upon the cumulative effects of several years of good nutritional intake.

Another major factor which goes into the antler equation is the age factor. While it varies a bit in different areas of the country, a whitetail buck is generally not considered to be mature until he is $5\frac{1}{2}$ to $7\frac{1}{2}$ years old. That "half-year" is just about always thrown in, because most antler comparisons are made in the fall, when the antlers are fully developed. Since most fawns are born in late spring to early summer, they are a "half" year old in the fall.

At any rate, in order for a buck to grow his best set of antlers, whether they be typical or non-typical, he must first reach maturity. Many bucks that do exhibit non-typical characteristics don't show these non-typical tendencies at an early age. While there are no reliable rules, it's fairly common for non-typical points to show up for the first time on a buck during his fourth or fifth set of antlers, and sometimes even later. I'm aware of quite a number of examples in which major non-typical characteristics showed up for the first time at eight or nine years of age. Sometimes there are exceptions with younger bucks, and you do occasionally see 1½ to 3½-year-old bucks with non-typical points, but the extra points are usually not particularly significant. However, these young bucks should be watched closely. There is some indication that at least a few of the true "super-bucks" begin to show their stuff early on, and there are examples of 3½-year-old bucks in the Boone and Crockett record book.

With experience in observing whitetails, you may in time begin to be able to look at a buck and make a reasonable guess of his antler potential, but this is far from an exact science, even for the best biologists. There will always be some bucks which will completely defy accurate definition. Here's one example.

On a large ranch where a whitetail management program had been implemented, there was a specific buck which was observed and judged to be approximately 4½ years old. He had nice antlers, but not spectacular. He seemed to have attained mature body weight and he had eight all-typical points with a slightly larger than average antler

When good nutrition, excellent genetics and full maturity all come together, the results can be most impressive. This buck was thought to be approximately 6½ years old and possibly in his prime.

When a buck accidentally damages his antlers while they are in velvet and still growing, and the tines try to grow some more, the points sometimes become blunted and knobby. The results are frequently called "acorn points." The buck on the left has four "acorn points." The young buck on the right has a highly unusual set of antlers. The reason for the antler growth on his forehead is unknown. I only saw him once, and I couldn't see any signs of injury. The world of antlers is filled with mysteries.

When I first saw this yearling buck, I thought his pedicle was broken and flopping down. However, as I watched further it became apparent that the antler was sturdy and growing in that fixed position. Could it be a birth defect, or maybe a severe head injury?

frame. His only unusual characteristic was his exceptionally long and heavy browtines, perhaps nine inches long.

The next year this same buck showed up at the same waterhole, sporting a large drop-tine, well out on his right beam. He was described to everyone on the ranch, and it was decreed that he would be protected from hunters. It was hoped that he would survive and function as a breeding buck, just in case there was a genetic connection to his major non-typical look.

Another year passed, and he was again observed carrying the large drop-tine on his beam. He had also added an eight-inch "sticker" point, which aimed backwards, as well as another sticker point, a double brow-tine (still huge), and an additional typical point. He went from an almost "average" eight-pointer to a spectacular 13-point non-typical in two seasons. The reason why is not known. He didn't exhibit any signs of injury. The only thing that had obviously changed was his age. He went on to become one of the more dominant bucks in that area of the ranch. He was seen from time to time over the next several years. During this time his antlers varied, but they were always non-typical.

One fall a hunter reported seeing "Ol' Drop-kick" from his blind, and the old buck had been in a crippled, emaciated state. The rancher hunted the buck for almost two weeks before he finally found and harvested him. He was in such a weakened condition that his death was imminent. At the time of his demise, he was probably 11½ years old, based on the years of observation by the rancher and his family. That in itself is remarkable for a wild deer. Most don't live nearly that long. His antlers were still extremely impressive. The inside spread measured 25 inches, there were two major droptines (one on each beam) and he carried 15 points.

I was able to find and photograph this buck for three years but he became exceedingly reclusive and secretive in his old age. Unfortunately, I wasn't able to find him at all during either of his last two seasons. At 10½, he was seen a couple of times by the rancher and was reported to have had triple droptines and 18 points.

The photograph on page 84 is a shot I took from a blind, when his age was estimated to be 7½. He was a remarkable and interesting deer.

I have yet another excellent example of the difficulty involved in predicting what kind of antlers a buck will grow. An older gentleman with whom I am acquainted once had a young whitetail buck which had taken up residence on his farm. The

This weird antler was probably caused by severe damage very early in the growth cycle. I believe I had seen "Ol' Paddlehead" the year before as a purely typical nine-pointer. He appears to be fully mature. I saw him again about two months later, and he had broken the "paddle" off, assumedly by fighting.

Bucks which have "typical" antlers can still have a wide variety of shapes and sizes. The buck on the right looks as though the long back tines of his arch-shaped rack are very nearly touching. The old-looking buck on the left not only has a strange set of gnarly 5x7 typical antlers, with beams that jut straight out, he also has a very unusual tail which is solid black on the top side.

buck was only a yearling, but even so he sported a very respectable 10-point set of typical antlers. As my friend enthusiastically waited to see what sort of antlers the buck would grow in his second season, he was very disappointed and bewildered when the buck only grew a typical eight-point rack the second year. There were no apparent nutritional problems and the genetic stock in the local area was deemed to be excellent. At any rate, my friend's disappointment was put to rest when the buck grew his third set of antlers. He grew a massive, 15-point non-typical rack. The buck stayed around the farm for years, and grew into one of the most impressive whitetail bucks I've ever seen. At age 7½ he exhibited extreme mass, 13-inch back tines and 20 points. The photo on page 85 was taken during October of that year.

One last example. A rancher friend with an extensive quality deer management program, had observed a young buck, 2½ years old, which already carried 10 substantial typical points along with several sticker points. The buck was protected from hunters (all hunts were guided) and that section of the ranch was carefully monitored to try to keep track of this very promising animal. Sure enough, he blossomed incredibly. By 4½ he already had 18 or 20 points, and by 5½, he was so big that it was supposed that he was probably at his prime. However, in the next year as he reached an estimated 6½ years, he made yet another quantum leap into the stratosphere of antler magic. As huge as he had been the previous year, virtually all aspects of his antlers increased in size by 25 percent or so. He had more typical points, more mass, more non-typical points, longer tine-length, wider spread — everything! See his photo on page 115.

This was a true "super-buck" in all respects. He had begun to show his stuff early in life, and then lived up to all expectations, and more. The situation was made more remarkable in that the rancher was able to observe and study this buck during his maturation process.

Whether the antlers are typical or non-typical, large or small, freakish or normal, they almost always come to the same conclusion after the rut winds down. When the time is right, the antlers are shed. The buck on the left has already cast off both antlers. The buck on the right is still holding onto one antler, even though it appears that the other has been gone for a while. Once in a great while a buck will not shed either his velvet or his antlers, usually as a result of an injury to his testicles.

In any event, attempting to predict the future antler potential of any particular buck is a pretty precarious business. More times than not, the young bucks which appear to be the most promising turn out to be only "nice" bucks, hardly ever the "super-bucks" you were hoping for. Oddly, in so many of the cases where "super-bucks" are observed or taken by hunters, it's the first time the buck has ever been seen. Such is the mysterious nature of truly large whitetails. They seem to appear and disappear with astonishing ease.

One other known cause for the formation of non-typical antlers can be an injury, either to the antler itself or a bodily injury to the deer. Injury to the antler itself may occur when the antlers are in velvet and growing. The buck may stumble and fall, striking his antlers on the ground. He may accidentally damage them going under a

When an antler falls off, an open, often bloody pedicle remains. There doesn't seem to be any appreciable pain or irritation associated with the process. It will quickly heal.

fence or through the brush. Bucks try to be very careful during this period but accidents do happen. This type of injury may simply result in crooked points or beams if they weren't hurt too badly. Occasionally this type of damage to points causes them to split into multiple points. Sometimes when the ends of the points are damaged, they attempt to continue growing, resulting in stunted or blunted points which are often called "acorn points." When antlers are damaged in velvet the damage is usually apparent only during that year, with the antlers returning to "normal" in subsequent years. However, in some cases, the antlers seem to "remember" the injury and re-grow in that damage-caused conformation in future years.

A different situation exists when a whitetail buck sustains a substantial bodily injury. A traumatic injury, particularly to the skeletal system, will almost inevitably result in the malformation of that buck's antlers in all future years. Studies have shown that the results are not entirely predictable. For example, a severe injury to a rear leg will usually cause the antler on the opposite side to be malformed in all years to come. In a small percentage of cases the antler malformation will be on the SAME side as the rear-leg injury. When a front leg is broken or damaged, the result is generally different. Oddly enough, when a front leg is hurt, it is usually the antler on the SAME side as the injury which becomes malformed. Again, a small percentage does the opposite.

These injury-related antlers relate to our non-typical interest because these antlers virtually never grow out in "typical" fashion

I was really surprised when I first saw this buck at a distance. As he got closer I could see that he had lost the lower part of his left rear leg. He seemed fairly mature and in good condition overall. The leg was healed, but he couldn't put any weight on it. He hopped very awkwardly, with that left leg gyrating as though he was riding a stationary bicycle but when he spooked and ran, he moved like the wind. As in most cases with major rear-leg injuries, the opposite antler was affected.

A sight like this will take your breath away. This is the kind of whitetail that can make you weak in the knees ...a fully mature, non-typical "super-buck". It's hard to imagine how he could carry the weight of all that bone on his head. He would easily make the Boone and Crockett record book. The mature buck on the left is actually quite large, but he is literally dwarfed by the big deer.

again. There is a possibility that some "non-typical" antler characteristics could be related to an injury or physical defect which might not be apparent. There's no proof of this, but it's an interesting thought. Whitetails are extremely resilient creatures, and are capable of surviving incredible injuries. I briefly mentioned, earlier in this book, a rancher friend who had accidentally cut both front legs off a whitetail fawn while mowing hay. The fawn stumbled off, on the stubs of his knees, assumedly to perish, but he didn't. The fawn not only survived the grotesque accident but was seen on the ranch for many years, leading a normal life, except of course for his lowered front end. He always had a head full of non-typical antlers, not of heroic proportions, but never typical. When he died at the approximate age of 9½, his teeth were completely

worn out, and he had 15 points with beams that curved downward. He had callous pads about four or five inches thick on the stubs of his front legs. Whitetails survive so successfully with serious injuries, it's easy to imagine that they might cope with more minor physical defects in such a fashion that we would never even be aware of the defects.

The giant non-typical "super-buck" that lives in many dreams does exist, but he's a truly rare animal. The more you look into and consider all the factors which go into his creation, the more you realize that he will probably always be exceedingly rare, in spite of the best efforts of deer managers and biologists. There's hardly a more spectacular sight in the animal kingdom than that of a mature white-tailed "super-buck."

It's easy to see that the small buck in this photo is a yearling. The 12-pointer is mature. Note the size differences in virtually all aspects of their appearances. Every dimension is noticeably different.

Notice the slender features of the buck on the left, compared to the older deer on the right. The mature buck shows some bulges and curves that the younger buck just doesn't have. Give him a couple of years and he will.

There are three different age classes represented in this photo. The middle buck is 2½ years old, the buck on the right is 3½ and the deep-chested buck on the left is likely to be 5½ or more.

BIG BUCKS? or LITTLE BUCKS?

If managing for the biggest bucks possible is your goal, there's an important lesson in this photograph. Each of these bucks carries 11 points on good-sized mainframes. They're both wide-racked, 21 to 22 inches inside the beams. However, the similarities end there. One of them is much older than the other and has already made his contribution to the herd. He has also probably reached or even passed his prime. It is the buck on the left. He may be as old as 7½ or more. The buck on the right is estimated at 4½ years maximum. While his genetic antler potential appears promising, he probably hasn't done much breeding, as a subordinate buck.

Superficially, the question as to whether or not a buck is a "big" buck or a "little" buck might seem ridiculously easy and entirely self-evident. However, in the majority of field situations, the answer is not nearly so readily obvious. Even when some aspects are fairly obvious, the finer points of aging and judging relative antler size can be quite challenging.

To begin with, most people who pursue and study whitetails, particularly from a hunting standpoint, do so with a high level of emotional involvement. It is a very exciting endeavor, an adventurous ride on the time machine back to a simpler, more self-reliant time. It also involves ethics and logic, and possibly life and death. Responsible hunters want their decisions in the field to be informed and intelligent.

Whitetails are so secretive and elusive that pursuers spend most of their time waiting, watching, planning, studying, and just hoping to see one. It's commonplace to carry out your best-laid plans and wait anxiously for many hours (or even days), to finally see your quarry for only a very short time — maybe only seconds. These

The buck at the top of the page is an outstanding 2½-year-old. Even though he has sizable antlers, look at the slim lines of his face and body. The little buck below is a classic "long-yearling" ...1½ years old.

sightings often come suddenly, with little or no warning. The deer may be quite a distance away and the time factor is uncertain but likely to be brief. He may represent a poor opportunity, a good opportunity, or perhaps even a once-in-a-lifetime opportunity. The hunter must exercise all of his judgement and experience, under pressure, to gauge the situation.

Whitetail hunters are optimistic by nature. How else would you explain the almost universal willingness to keep going back out, morning after cold, wet morning when there may not have even been a sighting in days. Given this high level of optimism, that first glance at a new deer can be pretty tricky. The wait has been long and the time is short.

I don't mean to overrate the importance of large antlers, for hunters, or for others who observe and study whitetails. There are some people who don't give a hoot about whether a buck's antlers are large or small and that's fine. However, the truth is

that almost everyone involved in the study, observation, or hunting of whitetails uses the size of antlers as the primary yardstick in comparing or evaluating whitetail bucks. All these people are involved in the process of "field-judging" at one level or another, whether or not they originally intended to be. It's an almost inescapable part of basic hunting and a part of the identification process of the game being pursued. It would be virtually impossible to observe a whitetail buck, without noticing something about his aesthetic and/or measurable qualifications. This observation process evolves with experience, to the point where the practitioner may become very skillful with the complex judgements involved.

Accurately field-judging whitetail bucks in the wild is a difficult skill, one which you're not going to acquire overnight. It's both an art and a science; a matter of judging aesthetic qualities as well as quantitative information about the magnitudes of dimensions. To be objective, and to be

The buck at the top of the page is an excellent 3½-year-old. He's just beginning to get a little meat on his bones. The buck below is a very good 4½-year-old ...a little deeper, a little heavier throughout.

With 12 points, slightly non-typical features, and a very wide spread, this is a very handsome buck. I believe he is 5½ years old, judging from his body shape, his face and the way he interacted with a couple of other bucks. Also, I had seen him the previous year (see photo on page 117). He has excellent antlers but you should never try to judge a buck's age from his antlers.

good at it, requires a degree of emotional control which is well above and beyond the call of most duties. There are a lot of questions to be answered quickly. Are his antlers typical or non-typical? How many points does he have? How long are his tines? How wide is his antler spread? How massive are his antlers? How long are the main beams? What about his basal circumferences? How does he compare with most bucks in this geographic area? What is his age? How is his body condition?

As stated, good field-judgement is an acquired skill. You'll learn something about it in this chapter and in other writings, but it's a skill that for the most part can only be acquired through actual in-the-field experience.

The first big lesson in field-judging, for most deer hunters, usually comes as quite a surprise and often, a disappointment. The first time a hunter experiences the phenomenon known politely as "ground shrinkage" can be quite a shocking experi-

Sometimes when bucks are fully mature like both of the deer on this page, the concept of full maturity becomes quite obvious. The deep, heavy bodies and the full faces are the hallmarks.

No one could mistake the ancient character at the top of the page for a young deer. He's as old as Methuselah. The buck at the bottom is probably fully mature at 6½.

ence. The buck is one size at the time of the shot but hitting the ground apparently causes considerable antler shrinkage. By the time the hunter approaches, the antlers appear much smaller than they did on the standing animal. It defies all the laws of nature and physics, but if you don't believe it's true, just ask one of the thousands of people who've seen it happen.

Most hunters eventually recover from this first encounter with the now-dreaded "ground-shrinkage," though there may be a few that go to their graves convinced that some kind of magical switch took place. Most are able to come to terms with the fact that they simply made an error in judgement. They'll be more careful next time, more observant.

Then ...next time comes along. They remember what happened before, and they aren't about to go through that embarrassment and disappointment again. Be observant. Watch carefully. Here he comes. No problem this time. Everything is right.

There are times when you don't need to see a buck's face to know that he is fully mature. Just look at the body weight and the muscles on this monster 12-pointer. Look at that bulging neck! You won't see anything like that on a young deer. On top of that, he's having to turn his head sideways in order to thread his super-wide rack through the woods.

If tine-length gets you excited, then both of the bucks above should get your attention. While neither buck is particularly outstanding in other respects, both of them have tremendously long back tines, possibly as long as 15 or 16 inches. Both appear to be fully mature ...in fact, the buck at the top looks as though he might be "over the hill." He may be past his prime. Antler tines as long as these are quite rare.

After the shot comes the anxious approach to the prize, and incredibly, a surprising number of hunters have done it again — hapless victims of the "G" word. It's like a bad sequel to a bad movie, "GROUND-SHRINK II".

This is the time when some people begin to realize that there's more to this field-judging business than first impressions. Why did these hunters believe that the buck was bigger or better than he really was? It could be that some of them may not have actually seen very many deer, and they may not have much to go by. When you have a limited amount of one-on-one experience with deer in the woods, or if you're out there only very infrequently, there is a tendency for all bucks to look big. There's no question that the more experience you have actually watching deer in the wild, the better your field-judging potential will be. Eventually you can begin to get a feel for what the approximate norms are in your area, and consequently begin to be able to notice variances from the norms.

Sometimes there are also "ground-shrink" victims who are not inexperienced hunters. As mentioned, either hunting or studying deer is an emotional experience for many people. Even a little buck walking toward you in the woods is liable to increase your heart rate, and a nice handsome "average" buck is going to make your nervous system sing. Get a glimpse of a really good buck, and most folks get hit by an emotional cyclone. It's called "buck fever," and for the duration of its existence it can be seriously detrimental to your

judging ability, as well as your ability to concentrate, or even to breathe normally. With experience, and confidence, it eventually becomes a little more controllable, but it never really goes away completely. You do not have to be a hunter to get buck fever. It affects observers, naturalists, and photographers in exactly the same way.

After becoming more aware of the need for, and the complexities of, field-judging, many people begin to work on fine-tun-

Wide-antlered bucks usually make a very strong first impression, whether they have other strong antler characteristics or not. While they almost always look wider and more impressive when they're going away, they buck at the top is the real thing. Whitetails just don't get much wider than that. The "smaller" buck at the bottom is about 26 inches wide.

This is a gorgeous buck, and a very good example of what really long beams look like. Beam-length is one of the more difficult dimensions to accurately judge in the field.

ing their ability to properly judge whitetail bucks in the field. They're not looking for just "any" buck anymore. They want to be sure that they can tell the "good" bucks from the "bad" bucks.

Of course there are no bucks which are either inherently "good" or "bad." There are simply bucks with many different traits which can be recognized and compared. Most people are searching for a buck with traits which they personally find to be aesthetically pleasing. Naturally, most everyone is looking for the buck that "has it all," but considering the rarity of this almost mythical beast, the practical side of field-judging for most people is in searching for and being able to recognize particular characteristics which they prefer. A wide spread holds a fascination for some people, tall tines for others. Some prefer very symmetrical typical racks, while others would rather find a bizarre non-typical, even if it was smaller. Each person, over time, develops his own personal criteria as to what a "good" buck is. There are a great many different definitions of a "good" buck, and they are all correct.

Searching for a buck with a particular type of antlers usually amounts to two completely different challenges rolled into one. First, most people are looking for characteristics which are either rare or at the very least uncommon in the general population. Secondly, the types of characteristics usually pursued are normally present only on upper-age-class bucks, which make up only a very small percentage of most populations, and which by their experience level, are the most difficult animals to find.

Your antler judging ability in the field can be greatly enhanced by developing an ability to judge the approximate age of unknown bucks. This is not an exact science, and can be quite difficult, but it is a skill that can be developed. Knowing the approximate age-class of a buck can be valuable in helping to confirm or deny your judgement of his headgear. If you are comparing antler dimensions to body parts, it helps to have some idea whether you are comparing against the larger dimensions of a mature buck, or the smaller parts of a younger animal.

Aging bucks requires experience in the field and there is no single element which will give you the answer. Many characteristics have to be sized up individually, then collectively. In general, younger bucks will have relatively slender faces, with the lines of the nose and the jaw appearing as a fairly straight line. As they age, the nose becomes thicker, sometimes with a hump, and the jaw becomes fuller, perhaps a little droopy. The bodies of older deer are also thicker, and more muscular. The chest is deeper, the shoulders and hips wider. Also, more mature bucks tend to maintain an "attitude" in their body language which may help you to differentiate them.

There are a number of different yardsticks which are used in different areas in trying to determine the dimensions of antlers. While some are of value as general guidelines, probably none are extremely reliable. In most cases, antler characteristics are compared to body parts such as ear-length, distance from ear-tip to ear-tip, nose-length, body-width, distance between antler bases, body-depth and so forth. Reliability is not consistent because these physical characteristics of deer can and do vary substantially. For instance, some bucks have an ear-tip to ear-tip measurement as small as 14 or 15 inches, while others can measure as much as 19 or 20 inches. This can greatly affect the estimated antler spread if a person is using this measurement for comparison. This method is still of value, because someone

Here is another example of a long-beamed buck. You can't readily tell from this angle, but he is also wide. This buck is not fully mature, most likely an up-and-coming 4½-year-old.

Mass is usually self-evident when it is present. Both of the two bucks above are well-endowed in the mass department. The surprising thing about these two deer is that they could exhibit such antler-mass when neither of them appears to be fully mature. The buck pictured below is quite the opposite. He is a good example of what some would call a "pencil-horned" buck.

who studies bucks in a particular area may be able to determine that it is common for bucks in his area to have an ear-tip spread of approximately a certain amount. It is common in many areas for this measurement to be approximately 16 to 17 inches ...but don't always bet on it. It can vary substantially in the same local area.

There are a few other general guidelines which may help you in your field-judging endeavors. For example, you can rarely tell very much about a buck with only one view, head-on for instance. To be very accurate, you really need more than one view to work from. Almost every buck has at least one angle from which he appears to be larger than he really is.

Whitetail bucks which are walking or running directly away from you have a tendency to appear much larger than they actually are. In most cases the buck is aware of your presence, and has his ears

These two photos of the same buck show just how difficult it can be to judge from a single view. He has 13 well-developed points, and in the above view he looks quite impressive. However, seen head-on, you get a different impression.

aimed back toward you, tight against the sides of his head. This causes his spread to seem much wider than actual. Also, with the ears tucked back, the overall rack will seem larger compared to the now seemingly smaller head. In addition, many times he will have his neck stretched high, especially if running. This too creates an illusion of larger and taller antlers in relation to the rest of the body.

Observing a buck in the fog, or in the low light levels of early morning or late afternoon can be very deceiving. One reason may be that your ability to judge distance can be greatly impaired under these conditions. Also, under these conditions, many points of reference which you might otherwise use or relate to, are partially or totally obscured from your vision. Not to be underrated in these situations is the

tendency for one's imagination to work double-time when visibility is poor. It's a good time to proceed very cautiously.

Good field-judgement capabilities are essential for the most beneficial management of whitetails. Once management objectives have been determined, then biologists, wildlife managers, and hunters can use their field-judging abilities to determine which animals should be removed from the herd, and to evaluate the status of the population dynamics.

The overall consensus from hunters, biologists, naturalists, and wildlife managers is that it's much more exciting to see mature bucks with big antlers, than to see only young deer. The only way to make

The two photos on this page illustrate another example of a buck which looks different from different angles. Seen at a distance in the shot above, he appears to be quite good. However, when he approached my blind and came into close-range, head-on status, the look was very different.

this more possible, from a management standpoint, is to protect and/or not harvest the young and middle-aged bucks. Obviously, if a buck is harvested at age 2½, with a small or average set of antlers, he will never be observed at age 5½, carrying what might possibly have been an outstanding set of antlers. Field judgement is the primary tool which makes it possible to differentiate and selectively control harvest which is a key component of management.

Another benefit in learning to properly judge whitetails in the field, is that you will begin to see the tremendous individuality within the herd. It forces you to notice specific details, which you might have never noticed before. For instance, did you

These two photos of the same buck were taken two years apart. In the smaller picture, he was probably 3½ years old and had very average looking antlers. Due to the whitetail management practices on the ranch where I found him, under which young and middle-aged bucks were protected, he grew into a very impressive 5½-year-old buck.

ever realize how recognizable individual whitetail faces can be? Or how distinctive their personalities can be? Individual whitetails are usually as recognizable by their faces and other specific characteristics ...as is your uncle Charlie or your cousin Bob. You'll begin to recognize deer from year to year, more by their faces, body shapes, and personalities than by their antlers. You'll be amazed by what you learn in making these distinctions. While there is a certain satisfaction in simply knowing that there are anonymous deer living in the woods generally, there is a distinctly higher level of satisfaction in the certain knowledge that there are particular, individual deer living there.

Comparative measurements and scoring systems are not for everyone, but used sensibly, they can provide interesting information and convenient points of reference, for both field-judging and communication with others who study or hunt whitetails. For most people, the overall aesthetics of a particular set of antlers will be the deciding factor as to whether or not they judge a buck to be "good" — at times overriding measurement considerations. To a large and very important extent, "BIG" and "GOOD" will always be defined in the eye of the beholder.

I photographed the wild buck on these two pages for five consecutive seasons on a remote ranch. It's very unusual for me to be able to find, let alone photograph, any wild buck for five years in a row. They usually get taken by hunters, die of natural causes or simply just disappear, never to be seen again. Some years I didn't see much of him, but he had a very recognizable face and personality, and it was easy to tell it was him each time I found him again. I began calling him "Amber-Eyes" after seeing him the first time. He did indeed have amber-colored eyes, which were quite unlike the normal dark-brown to black eyes which most whitetails have. They were particularly noticeable when the sun shone on his face, making his eyes seem almost translucent.

He is one of about six different bucks which I've seen, in different areas and at different times, all of which had translucent amber-colored eyes. It apparently is quite a rare characteristic. In the first photo at the top left, he was assumed to be 2½ years old (which was confirmed when he was tooth-aged after his demise at 6½). The lower small picture on the left shows him at 3½. The first large photo on the left was taken when he was 4½. The middle large photo (above left) shows him at 5½, with incredibly long tines. This particular set of antlers was found after they were shed, and the back tines were 15 inches long. The last photo (above right) shows him with a drop-tine and 27-inch beams at age 6½.

When I first saw the 12-pointer in the small lower-right photo from my blind, I couldn't remember ever having seen him before, even though I knew the area extremely well. Then I realized that he was only 2½ years old. From that day on I called him "Super-Buck" as he appeared to have great potential. Sure enough, I found him again for the next two years at the same blind and he did grow up to be what I would consider a super-buck. He was very handsome as a 3½-year-old (upper left photo), but at 4½ he was incredible. At the time of this photo, it appeared that he had already broken off several points from fighting, yet he still had at least 16 points. He was very dominant toward the other deer in the area.

The series of photos on this page illustrates four years in the life of a super-wide buck. In the first photo at the top left, this buck was quite ordinary, and had an antler spread of 16 or 17 inches. I had rattled him up for the photo. He appeared to be 2½ years old. In the middle small photo, he made a quantum leap at the age of 3½. The spread of his antlers jumped out to 23 or 24 inches. In the small photo at the bottom right, at 4½ he added mass and a little more spread. He was a sucker for the "horns" ...I had rattled him up again. As you can see in the large photo, he was quite impressive at age 5½. He only had nine points, but on a tremendous frame about 26 inches wide. As a dominant buck he was jealously guarding his doe.

Whitetails are beautiful to observe in many situations, but there are few sights as impressive as a mature whitetail buck making a big jump. Such a streamlined display of strength and control would make a champion gymnast envious but for the whitetail making the jump it's really nothing at all. He does it as effortlessly as you or I might step over a low curb.

CATCH HIM IF YOU CAN

Whitetails are unbelievable athletes. Not only do they move with great speed and agility, through all sorts of habitat and around or over all manner of obstructions — they do it with incredible grace. This photo of a buck running full-out was taken by setting the shutter speed on the camera to a very slow speed and then following the running buck very precisely with the camera. It's called a "panning" shot, and is one of the more difficult types of photos to do well.

Before you can hear "the call of the whitetail" — before you can begin to study their intelligence, or behavior, or check out the magic of antlers — you have to be able to find and see whitetails. Whether observing whitetails for study purposes, for personal relaxation or to put meat in the freezer, you've got to be able to find them first.

In the beginning it can be a formidable task. There are a multitude of gyrations to go through, just to find lands which might harbor whitetails. You can talk to wildlife agencies and to chamber-of-commerce personnel in areas where whitetails live generally. Talk to ranchers, farmers, barbers and candlestick-makers ...anybody who'll listen who might have a clue as to where there could be lands with deer.

After you've uncovered a few possibilities, you'll have to contact the proper agencies if it's public land, or landowners if it's private land, to try to get permission to gain access. In many cases this accessibility will not be available, and in the cases

To see whitetails, you first have to find them. It sounds simple enough, but you just never know exactly where they're going to be. The speedster above has just bolted from beneath a bush in the middle of a large open pasture. It seemed an unlikely place for a big buck like this to be hiding, but such situations aren't all that unusual.

While I was diligently trying to spot whitetails, I was lucky to spot this bedded buck with my binoculars. All those points aren't nearly so visible from a distance.

where it is, there may be a fee charged. There are likely to be rules and/or regulations, and it's very important that you follow them all to the letter. After all, this is only the beginning of your whitetail quest. Without basic access to lands which harbor whitetails, you will have no opportunity whatsoever to accomplish your goals. Such access should never be taken for granted. When a private landowner grants you the access to enter his property, even if you're paying for the right, it should be considered a major "gift." The fact that he is sharing something personal with you must never be overlooked. He and his property must be treated with the utmost respect, if a good relationship (and continued access) is to be maintained.

Gaining access to good whitetail country is the first major step in your quest for whitetails. Once you've cleared that high hurdle, you can start trying to figure out

What a buck! I only wish that he had stayed a little longer. It's amazing that you can go to such lengths and so much effort to try to work out complicated ways to get close to deer ...and then you see a buck like this while driving across a ranch in a pickup.

where the deer are. Begin by asking the landowner about the history of whitetails on his property, and in the local area. Ask about details of whitetails previously seen there, or previously taken by hunters.

After you've learned everything you can from the landowner, you must get out in the field and begin to look for sign, any sign that there have ever been any deer on the property at all. By looking for and finding deer droppings, trails or rubs, you can establish that there have been whitetails there at some time in the recent past. You'll want to survey the property thoroughly in order to try to understand how whitetails are using it. Walk the creeks and ravines and their edges to try and uncover any travel patterns. Check out the fence-rows for crossings. Look in areas of more dense brush for signs of bedding activity. See if you can determine any of the prima-

It takes practice and effort to develop a good eye for seeing whitetails in their native habitat. This buck's huge antlers wouldn't be nearly so easy to see if I hadn't zeroed in on him for you with the camera. At a distance, they would blend with the brush.

This heavy-horned 10-pointer is heading back down into a creek, which he was using for cover. He traveled a good distance in the bottom of the creek and then re-emerged.

ry feeding habits of the local deer. Learn where the foods are and where the deer must go for water. If you get lucky, maybe you'll find a shed antler or two. There's plenty of detective work to be done.

Once you've learned a little about the local whitetail population, and begun to understand how the deer are using the property, you have to formulate a plan as to how you might actually see and get close to them. You might decide to elevate yourself in a tree stand or tower stand, for increased visibility. This also positions you out of the usual line-of-sight of whitetails traveling through the area and helps with scent dispersion. You may decide to build a blind on the ground, either from wood, or from brush and natural materials. When the times and conditions are right, you may just decide to dress in full camouflage, and back into a bush at a major crossing or water hole.

When still-hunting in the woods , you must assume that there is a buck behind every bush, tree and log. If you're not extremely careful, the first time you let your guard down and decide there are no deer around, you might be faced with a scene like this.

The buck jumping the fence has super-long tines, and it looks like he has 12 or 13 points. While it seems that there wouldn't be much protection for him out here in the open, he has actually chosen his area pretty wisely. He can see potential threats at a considerable distance, and if anything begins to get close, he's just a short hop from the next pasture and the other side of the hill.

There are many ways to approach the challenge. In each case, you must take into account deer travel patterns, wind directions, and whitetail motivations, whether they be feeding, drinking, bedding, or breeding. It's a good idea to have several options set up and available in order to take advantage of changing conditions.

There are many different exciting and adventurous ways of pursuing whitetails. One of the most interesting, and at the same time one of the most demanding in terms of skillfulness and knowledge, is "still-hunting." Still-hunting is perhaps the most basic method of hunting. It is the art of stalking through the woods, very slowly and very quietly, using available natural cover and wind and light, attempting to sneak within close range of the quarry. It requires patience, skill, and stealthiness, and the hunter's ability to see and discern hidden deer is of the utmost importance.

Whitetails learn about getting away at a very young age. This young super-athlete has no trouble at all clearing a fence that is three times as tall as he is.

Like a streamlined projectile, this August-antlered buck sails over the fence as smoothly as the wind. Not only do fencerows help define travel patterns, but they also offer some degree of protection to whitetails, who can so easily cross to the other side, leaving predators or pursuers grappling with the need to go through, over, under or around them.

Even seeing whitetails which are not hiding can be quite a challenge at times. From a distance this big buck's colors would blend right in as he traveled up the brushy hillside.

The experience of sneaking up on a wild whitetail in the woods produces a great sense of satisfaction, and with good reason ...it's a rare experience. For each success, there will be countless other times when you also did most of the right things but for a myriad of reasons, the end result was not the same. For a hunter, stalking a buck successfully is a goal which can be achieved occasionally, but which can never be mastered completely.

What hunter who has stalked through the deer woods can honestly say that he or she has never been "had" by a nice whitetail buck ...and not just once, but probably many times? Think about it. You've just executed your stealthiest most perfect sneak through the brush, noiselessly, into the wind. Everything's perfect, and you've just spent 20 minutes motionless in one spot, surveying every nook and cranny of the woods around you. You decide with

*This whitetail must surely be in the middle of a 30-foot leap. Maybe longer. I was walking across the hillside when I apparently jumped him out of his bed. So many times you come across whitetails while traveling to the places where you **thought** you would find them. This buck was greatly alarmed by my presence, and made several of these tremendous bounds on his way out.*

confidence that there are NO deer in the immediate vicinity. It's time to move slowly onward. As you take the first careful step, a whitetail buck explodes out of a bush 10 yards back and 30 yards over. What went wrong? Simple, you didn't SEE the deer! Countless variations of this scenario are played out each year.

Naturally, we have our physical visual limitations. Sometimes it's virtually impossible to see the deer. However, there's more to "seeing" deer than you might imagine. To begin with, most people are too willing to accept what they see at first glance, as absolute fact. In order to be more successful at seeing deer we have to learn to automatically question everything we see, and then to question it again, to be sure. Each object is debated by the eyes, the brain and the imagination. The eyes locate an object ...the imagination calls it a deer ...the brain calls it a stump. The eyes

Try to imagine how difficult it was to see this big, wide-antlered buck at a distance, when the entire hillside looked like this. When he heard the truck, he froze, thinking he would not be seen.

Edge habitat, where two or more types of habitat or vegetation converge, is a favorite hangout for whitetails. "Edge" areas provide a wider diversity of resources for deer to utilize, than the more monotonous habitats on either side, where the options are more limited. This photo of a huge buck working his way down a brushline is a classic example of edge utilization.

quickly search for any collaborating evidence, a slight movement, a partial profile, a little reflection from an antler or nose — anything that might help make identification positive. Also, there's a real time crunch, just in case it's a real deer. Real deer don't usually wait around nearly as long as "stump-deer" do.

Naturally, the easiest deer to see are deer which are moving. Even a small amount of movement, the twitch of an ear or tail, or the turning of a head, make the locating of a deer many times easier than having to pick a motionless animal out of thick cover. Also, being able to see deer in motion is much more effective if the observer himself is stationary. This same principle holds true for the deer that may be motionless, watching you while you are moving through the woods. That's why it's

always a good idea to move very slowly, at a snail's pace, and to hug the cover and the shadows as much as possible. Unfortunately, most of the deer that are spotted as a result of their movement are moving at something just less than the speed of light when the observation is made. That's why it's important to learn to see deer **before** they're moving.

Whitetails are masters of concealment, and for them the concept of keeping a low profile is as automatic as breathing. Almost without effort, they seem to utilize every twig, every rock, every shadow to mask their presence. To be able to see whitetails before they see you, is a hard-earned skill. It usually comes only with practice, practice, and more practice.

Learning to "see" deer is an essential element in working towards your goal of find-

Here is another example of the use of edge habitat. This buck is traveling down the edge of a creek. The only problem is that he's just seen me and is waving goodbye with his flag.

ing and observing deer on a close-up basis. There are many, many nuances to be studied and analyzed. I could tell you all about looking for deer "parts," and the various ways of using light to your advantage, but far and away, the best way to improve your "deer eyes" will be to get out in the field and practice. Trial and error will be your best teacher.

Of all the different ways and styles of hunting and pursuing whitetails, there is one method which stands out as the unequivocal winner, where drama and suspense are concerned. For most people who have used the technique, there is nothing else that even approaches the excitement of successfully rattling up a buck. If you haven't tried it, you're missing out on the thrill of a lifetime. For newcomers to the technique, who are accustomed to watching whitetails with generally peaceful attitudes, it's a real shock and surprise when a

You should expect whitetails, especially older, more experienced deer to seek out some of the more inaccessible places in an area. I watched this mature buck climb a very steep hill to bed down on a high ridge where he felt secure.

Food plots can be excellent locations to find deer. The buck above is just coming out of the woods in late afternoon. It had rained the night before and the oat patch was soggy and full of water. Find where the preferred foods are and you'll find deer.

This bottomland buck has seen me as I was still-hunting through the woods. He has just jumped up from his bed.

buck comes charging in with his hair all bristled up and his nostrils flared. It's particularly impressive if this is happening at a distance of perhaps 10 yards, or even less in heavy brush. A whole new thought process begins when you realize that this buck is not just peacefully wandering in the woods, but instead, he's coming after YOU, with fire in his eye.

Of course they don't always come charging in. Many times bucks sneak in virtually unnoticed until they are suddenly in front of you. In fact, probably only a very small percentage of bucks which respond are ever seen by the hunter, particularly if the hunter is on the ground. More times than not the bucks are highly suspicious, and many times will circle downwind, scenting the hunter and leaving unseen.

This type of hunting can be full of surprises. One late morning, I carefully and slowly sneaked about 200 yards into a very dense brushy pasture, in an area where deer seemed to loiter and bed during the day. I carefully picked a spot between two bushes, and started a fairly gentle rattling sequence, just in case there was a buck in extremely close proximity. If so, the response is usually immediate.

Nothing happened. I began making as much noise with the antlers as possible, augmented by grunting and wheezing noises with my mouth and by kicking the brush with my foot. After a couple of minutes, I paused momentarily, to look in all directions. After I had quickly covered about 270 degrees, I thought I heard something behind me. I whirled to look. There was a small sapling about four or five yards behind me, that was springing back and forth in the wind. But there was NO wind. There was a wide-antlered buck bounding over the brush, heading away from me. Apparently he had been almost right on top of me, but I hadn't seen or heard him.

Some bucks prefer to stay in heavy cover. I got lucky with this one while still-hunting. I saw him before he saw me. When I took this photo, he heard the camera and that was the end of it.

I increased my odds of seeing a whitetail this day by sitting in a blind at a waterhole. There was a possibility of seeing deer coming to water. Also, the rut was on, and there was a chance that a buck such as this might be following doe-scent trails left by the does which had been watering there previously. This happened about the middle of the afternoon, as you can see by his shadow.

Even though he had seen me, and probably smelled me, I was able to coax him back out of the brush again by rattling the antlers. Ten minutes later he was standing broadside at about 30 yards.

Another time, in mid-afternoon, I sneaked up a brushy hillside and found a suitable spot. After a short, loud rattling sequence, I stopped and watched for a moment. I was camouflaged from head to toe and my back was well covered with

These two photos of the same buck were taken about 40 minutes apart. In the lower photo, I was camouflaged and watching a deer trail that went through the bottom of a deep ravine. It was late morning when the huge buck came down the trail. After he disappeared, I tried to circle around and find him again. There was a whole series of deep brushy ravines. Since I knew where the trail came out, and he never appeared, I felt sure he was hiding in one of the ravines. I couldn't seem to find him, but just as I was about to give up, I carefully peeked over the edge of a deep narrow ravine. He was standing there, hugging the wall. He had probably heard me as I stalked him and he was hiding. I got my camera ready and stepped up to the edge of the deep gully, and he exploded out the other side when he saw me. That's the photo on the left.

There are few things in this life that are more dramatic than being in close proximity to two mature whitetail bucks which are seemingly trying to kill each other. They metamorphose into wild-eyed demons, crazed beyond all reason, striking and lunging with incredible force. Sometimes it sounds more like a thrashing machine than a deer fight. It is much louder, and much more violent, than you might imagine.

One conclusion that I've drawn from this, which experience seems to have borne out, is that generally it is impossible to rattle too loudly or to make too much noise. It is physically impossible for you to hit the antlers together as forcefully as the real thing. The main exception to the "loud" rattling routine is the first rattling sequence in close, heavy brush when a buck might be very close.

For the best and most consistent results, it's important to sneak into, or along the edge of thick security cover. You'll have far more success coaxing a buck through

Rattling up whitetail bucks is surely the most exciting way to find deer. There's no other method of hunting whitetails that can compare to the drama and suspense of a big buck running towards you. The two photos on this page are typical successful rattling scenarios. The buck in the bottom photo is only 10 yards away.

the thick brush, where he feels secure, than you'll ever have getting him to cross even a small clearing. Certainly it's possible. I've seen them come in across 300-yard openings, but for more frequent success, go for the heavy brush.

I try to pay attention to wind direction when entering an area and setting up, and I frequently use a cover scent, such as skunk. But the truth is, I've had bucks come in from all wind directions on such a random basis, that it's tempting to discount the wind's importance. (I know it's heresy, but I've seen many bucks come running in from directly upwind, and count-less others from cross-wind.) Do the best you can with the wind. Above all else, it is essential that you **enter** the area completely undetected.

The type of antlers which you use to rattle with can vary tremendously and still be successful. I've rattled up many bucks with old, white, chalky sheds — in fact, with sheds of all sizes and descriptions. I've also successfully used various synthetic antlers, sticks (yes, sticks), and once even coaxed a nice buck out of the brush with two egg-sized rocks, because I had no "horns" and I could see him passing me by. I prefer fairly heavy, solid sheds, with the brow tines cut off. I don't soak them in magic potions or do anything special to them, other than cut off any excessive tine length. I don't really like using antlers which are too lightweight. You get too much "clickety-clack", and not enough "whoomp". At times you need that volume.

It's possible to rattle up a buck at virtually any time of the day. While it's tempt-

The photos on these two pages illustrate another exciting way to get close to whitetails. Deer decoys can work very effectively, either when used as a "doe," or when used as a "buck," with antlers attached. I've used decoys successfully many times, in a wide variety of locations and situations. The behavior elicited can be quite unpredictable, ranging from curiosity, to great interest, to confusion, to rage. Does fight with "doe" decoys, and bucks fight with "buck" decoys. Occasionally bucks mount and try to breed doe decoys, as in the example above. Decoys will work either with or without scent applied to them. Placement should be in a high-visibility location, as the visual cue is the main thing. One thing to note ...while deer are usually quite curious the first time out, they will usually remember and ignore the decoy completely if they see it again at a later date, even in a different location.

ing to say that the best times are early and late, my experiences have actually produced many of the **best** bucks in late morning and early afternoon. Go when you can, but keep in mind that if you rattle too much in any given area, the bucks will quickly become wise to you.

I've rattled up hundreds and hundreds of bucks (actually I'm probably well into four figures by now), and I'm still just like a kid at Christmas each time I set up to rattle again. The experience is so exciting, and so intense, and the results so unpredictable, that no one could ever tire of it. When it works, rattling antlers is one of the greatest shows on earth.

No matter which of the many methods you may use to pursue whitetail bucks you'll find him to be a more than worthy adversary. The whitetail is an amazing, adaptable animal. His main job is survival. For him it's a full-time job that he's been working on successfully for millions of years. He may be the best hide-and-seek player of all time. Just as you begin to figure out where to find him and how to see him, he reacts to the subtle pressures of encroachment, and he changes his schedules, hides in new places, and uses new concealment techniques. He's a hard man to catch.

Summertime whitetails have a very different look than fall and winter deer. They're also a little more laid back in their general attitudes during this period. I came upon this buck as I drove around a corner on a ranch road. I cut the engine and quickly took this photo with a big lens, while he was deciding whether I was friend or foe.

SEASONAL VIEWS

The Peaceful Season

One of the most interesting summer phenomenons is the formation of bachelor groups. Groups of three to five are common, and occasionally you may find groups of 10 or more. The five bucks in the top photo have been out feeding early on an August morning. Even though the sun is just barely up, they're already heading for the woods to bed down during the heat of the day. I located the three bedded bucks in the lower photo with my binoculars. It was a little unusual that they were lying in the sun.

These are all mature bucks. Don't let those small, slender "summer necks" fool you. Within 90 days or so after these photos were taken, their necks were probably twice as large, or more. It's just one of the amazing physiological changes which they go through. It always seems remarkable that they can carry those huge, blood-engorged velvet antlers with their tiny summer necks.

The small group of bucks in the top photo came out to start feeding, just before sundown. The "fur" of their velvet antlers catches the light, giving the appearance of being outlined in neon. In the bottom photo, the three bucks had been feeding around the pond since dawn. They're all looking toward the noise of a truck on a distant ranch road. A moment later, they spooked and ran away.

Most whitetail fawns are born in late spring and early summer. It seems that they practically hit the ground running. By the time they are just a few weeks old, like the one in the lower photo, they've already become very quick on their feet. Does very commonly have twins. Notice in the top photo how much larger one twin is than the other. The buck fawns put on size more quickly than the doe fawns.

When summer conditions have been good and everything is lush and green, the deer get to lead an easy life for a while. The two young bucks above had been grazing peacefully on the flower-covered hillside, when they were startled by some livestock coming over the hill to the left. They weren't alarmed for long. They fed for a few more minutes and left to bed down for the day.

During the heat of the summer, whitetails spend more time around water than usual. Having noticed a lot of deer sign at this water hole, I sat in a blind here for a number of mornings, with some success. These two very good bucks had just come to water, when a ranch hand came down the road toward the pond, not realizing I was there. That ended my photo shoot for the morning.

The top photo, taken in the wild, shows a large whitetail bachelor group. There were 9 or 10 bucks in the group, as well as a couple of does, which is a bit unusual. The group was made up of various age classes, and there were two bucks which were quite large. The big buck in the bottom photo is a beautiful example of a late August buck in all his splendor.

As the end of summer nears, and early fall approaches, whitetail bucks begin to get a little edgy with each other. As you can see in the top and right photos, dominance behaviors become more pronounced. The bucks don't want to hit their velvet antlers, so they work it out in other ways. The lower left photo shows the changing of the summer coat in progress. Out with the red and in with the gray.

All bucks do not remove the velvet from their antlers at the same time. The process is usually spread out over a two to three-week period. About half of the bucks in the bachelor group in the top photo have removed their velvet. A warm early fall created the unusual picture for the bottom photo. It's unusual to see a hard-antlered buck standing in blooming sunflowers.

As early fall begins, and all the bucks get their velvet off, their personalities begin to change as their testosterone level increases. Nevertheless, it's a gradual process, and some of the bachelor groups still hold together for a while, even after the velvet is gone. With every passing week they become more and more agitated, and the bachelor groups soon break up altogether.

After the first few weeks of fall have passed, the bucks have broken up and begun all the ritual processes of the pre-rut period ...rubbing, scraping, licking branches, etc. They're in their best physical condition of the year and are really starting to feel their oats. The big-bodied, mature buck above is a good example. He's muscled-up, primed and ready to go.

As the time for the rut approaches, bucks begin moving around more and more, in an effort to broaden their territories and to predominate as much as possible. Mature bucks start traveling to places which are sometimes long distances from their usual travel patterns. You can see from his silhouette, that this buck is mature. He's working a scrape line on the edge of a creek.

As bucks become more and more active with the approaching rut, you may begin to see them moving at almost any time of the day. Also, about this time, a few of the older, more secretive bucks may inadvertently show themselves for the first time of the season. It can be amazing how big bucks that have never been seen before seem to come out of the woodwork during the rut.

As the more mature bucks are traveling around establishing their dominant presence as widely as possible, they begin to get caught out in the open more frequently, like the buck in the top photo. Some of the younger bucks, like the 2½-year-old in the bottom photo tend to get a little ahead of the game. They sometimes begin rushing the does a little prematurely.

Fall has come and woe be the buck who crosses the path of the behemoth above. He's a full-blown, dominant, mature buck with a bad attitude. He was more or less standing guard over a doe group which was browsing in the creek bottom. He seemed to be spoiling for a fight. Another semi-mature buck approached the area and this buck had his antlers in the other's rump for a hundred-yard chase.

Finally, the rut is on, and big bucks are appearing out of nowhere, searching for receptive does. The high-tined buck trotting through the frost-covered weeds in the top photo is hot on the heels of a doe. I watched him chase her all over the open pasture, blowing smoke in the cold early morning air. The buck at the bottom has his nose to the ground, hot on the trail of a doe.

With the rut in full swing, you can find bucks performing all kinds of behaviors, including scent-rubbing, scraping and performing the flehmen behavior. The buck in the above left photo was jealously guarding a doe, but took time out to vigorously rub the pine tree about 10 yards from her. The buck in the large photo below is tasting the grass where a doe has urinated.

It's time, and both of the bucks on this page are in hot pursuit of does which are either in or near estrus. Both are mature, muscled-up, and in great body condition. It's a good thing, because after 60 days of running and chasing, and fighting and rutting, they will likely lose at least 30 percent of their body weight. Maybe more.

There's no time like the rut for seeing big bucks. Caution is often thrown to the wind, if it interferes with their single-minded objective. I was walking down the fencerow in late morning, when I took the top photo. A doe bolted out of the brush on the right and went under the fence to the left. The huge buck that was with her had no choice but to go over the fence after her. Another time, he might have held tight and gone unnoticed. The buck on the bottom chased does all morning long out in a wide-open pasture.

Big bucks like this appear as though by magic during the rut. As you can see by this example, rattling antlers can be very effective, during this period, if you can find a buck that's not with a doe. It's usually very difficult to persuade them to leave a doe but if there are bucks on the prowl, in-between encounters, they can be easy marks.

If you're looking for bucks during the rut, all you have to do is find the does. Find the does, and the bucks will never be far away. This group of does was gathered at a feeding station near my blind. I knew that the buck coming over the fence would probably not be interested in eating. He rushed several of the does to get a reaction and then singled one out and chased her out of sight.

After the rut begins to wind down, the seriousness of survival bears down on whitetails everywhere. The deer of the far north have to contend with the numbing cold, and it can be brutal, but even the deer in the more moderate climates have a serious challenge to face. Many mature bucks get so run down by the rut, that they just don't survive.

Whether there's snow on the ground or not, the times of easy living for whitetails are over when winter arrives. Whitetails tend to congregate in groups during these times, drawn to whatever meager foodstuffs may be available. The large group of deer in the top photo has been drawn together by the plowed-under crop field. The pickings may be slim, but they'll search out every morsel.

It seems that there's never enough food for whitetails during the winter. That they survive winters at all is testament to the hardiness of the species. Some actually do quite well. Just look at the buck in the lower left. He seems to be in great condition. On the other hand, look at the buck in the lower right. He's been reduced to eating foods that will not sustain him. He is starving to death.

The group of deer in the top photo has gathered at a beat-down, frozen oat patch. It may not be much, but when there's nothing else, it will draw deer from around the countryside like a magnet. The mature, once-heavy-bodied buck in the lower left has lost so much weight from the rigors of the rut that his bones are showing. As seen in the lower right, sometimes they just don't make it.

One of the keys to getting whitetail photos like this, is in the simple fact of being in the right place when the right times come around. Since such a thing is almost impossible to predict, a photographer's job is to scout around and find some of the right places. Then, you can only succeed by "being there" a lot, so that when one of those "right" times comes around, you'll be there to get the shot. Ninety-nine percent of the time is spent planning and waiting, and one percent is spent frantically trying to get the picture.

THE STORY BEHIND THE PICTURES

Frequently, when people see a photo such as this, there are comments about how remarkable it was that he "posed" for me so well. I take no offense, but nothing could be further from the truth, either for this particular photo or for so many others which are seen in that way. The majority of the better shots are split-second opportunities, taken under pressure, after planning, hoping and waiting.

Wherever I go to give presentations on whitetail behavior, whitetail photography or just on whitetails in general, people always have a lot of questions. Above all else, they want to know two things. **Where** did I get those pictures? And **How** did I get those pictures?

The "where" part is relatively easy to answer, because the answer is that I can't say. A very significant factor in my work is that I cannot divulge the locations where my photographs are taken. Much of the work is done on private lands and an important part of my job is to zealously guard the privacy of the people who have so graciously granted me access.

In a broader sense, I can tell you that I've photographed whitetails in possibly as many as 60 to 70 different locations in a half-dozen states and Mexico. Since I live in Texas, and the Texas deer herd and habitat is so diverse, a major portion of my work is done there. Nevertheless, I have spent a substantial amount of time with northern whitetails, mid-western whitetails, and deer of the deep south.

Overall, the procurement of access to lands with potentially outstanding whitetails is a most difficult task. People gener-

With whitetail photography you work hard, you plan, and you get out there and hope for the best. There are all kinds of combinations of luck and skill involved. Where this type of work is involved, it often seems that it would be better to be lucky than good. I was very lucky to see the buck in the above photo, but it wasn't so lucky in that the only way I could get the picture was to shoot it "offhand" with a heavy 500mm lens. The best luck of all was that I got away with such a questionable practice on this occasion.

ally are very concerned and secretive about their properties, and rightfully so. Now that I have a more well-known reputation, and so much awareness of my published works, access is not the problem that it was in the beginning.

The "**How** did you get those pictures?" question has a somewhat more complicated answer than the "Where?". Regardless of all the photos you see in this book, and in other publications, whitetails are exceedingly difficult to photograph well. It takes expensive equipment, thorough knowledge of the equipment and photographic principles, extensive knowledge of the animals and a willingness to go to great extremes

of discomfort and inconvenience to get the job done. There is far more effort involved in most good whitetail photography than the average observer might imagine.

First, before anything else can be done, comes the task of determining proper equipment and learning the myriad nuances of operating it correctly under stressful circumstances. This in itself is no small thing, but I'm going to avoid the flood of technical questions at this time. Entire books have been written about the technical matters alone. For the curious, I will say that all my primary equipment is made by Canon and I've been generally pleased with it. I basically use Canon F-1

The only way a photographer can come up with shots like this is to be there, morning after morning. As you can see by the position of the sun in the photo, it was very questionable whether there would be a visible sunrise at all, with the cloud bank moving in. The buck was gone and the clouds covered the sun within moments. The opportunity below was equally brief.

cameras with motor drives, and various Canon telephoto lenses, primarily the 200mm (F2.8), 300mm (F2.8L), 400mm (F4.5), and most of all the 500mm (F4.5L). My exposures are set by hand, rather than automatic. I don't use any specialized filters, but do try to be in the right places when the natural light and colors are at their optimum. If I'm photographing from a blind, I use a heavy Gitzo tripod, but I also frequently take off cross-country and shoot offhand. Most of my photographs are taken with Kodachrome-64 slide film. While this is a mixed bag of information, it covers many of the first questions which are usually asked of me about equipment.

There's quite a lot of study and practice necessary, before you can reasonably expect to pick up a heavy 500mm-equipped camera, go into the woods, and

Opportunities such as these are always fleeting, so you can never let your guard down when watching deer. Shots such as these are rarely available for more than a second or two.

hope to come back with high-quality photographs of any kind, let alone high-quality photographs of whitetail deer. It takes a lot of trial-and-error, and a great deal of time spent studying results. Even after all that, the hardest part is yet to come.

Easily, the most difficult thing about photographing whitetails is the whitetail himself. The nature and life-styles of whitetails are simply not conducive to most photographic needs. As you certainly know by now, they're exceedingly shy and reclusive, making them hard to find in the first place. When they are found, they're as excitable and spooky as they were shy and reclusive. Further, they tend to move very early and very late, and much of their most interesting activity occurs at times when the light is poor and extremely marginal for photography. So many times I've waited patiently for hours, finally to have a nice buck show himself for the first time just minutes after the light level has fallen too low. If only you could see all the photographs that I couldn't quite get!

Just because you can find a buck, does not mean you can photograph him. So many things can, and do, go wrong. It seems he's always too far away, or running through thick brush, or in the wrong direction for the light. There are countless "photo-spoilers" in the deer woods — the lone stick in front of his face, the unwanted fence in the background, the untimely appearance of a ranch hand coming over the hill, the unexpected rain shower, etc. On those rare occasions when you do seem to have a buck in a photographable position, then "Murphy" usually steps in and zaps your camera, or your film, or a wild hog or coyote barrels out of nowhere to run your subject off. Everybody's heard of Murphy's Laws, but it's only with whitetail photography that you learn the true extent of Murphy's sadistic tendencies. I've even taken a few truly great photos of whitetails

Some shots are not based so much on action, or behavior, as just on the pure beauty of the animals and the conditions. It's not often that such an opportunity exists, when the animals are prime and mature and the early morning light is pretty close to perfect. These two bucks, standing in the edge of the early morning light, were staring at a third buck which was approaching.

without any film in the camera at all. It's always something!

At this point, I'd estimate that I have probably photographed between 1,200 and 1,500 different whitetail bucks, mostly in the wild, and to tell you the truth, I can't remember any of them as being "easy." Some were harder than others, but there are so many variables that have to come together for the success of a whitetail photo, that sometimes I'm amazed that any of them work at all.

Generally, it seems that the best whitetail photography is accomplished as a solitary venture. I've worked in the company of others on several occasions and I found those experiences very pleasurable, but for most wild whitetail photography, it's just not the most practical approach for the optimum results. Too many things can go wrong with only one person working, and

the risks are usually magnified when others are involved. Beyond that aspect, I'd have a hard time asking others to go and assist me, simply because it would be asking too much. I go through too many extreme efforts and circumstances to ask someone else to do that. Persistence is frequently the name of the game. A whitetail photographer has to get out there and try whether it's extremely hot or cold, raining, blowing, snowing, uncomfortable, inconvenient or whatever. Such extreme working conditions are the rule rather than the exception, and they must be taken in stride if successful whitetail photography is the objective. A photographer must be utterly relentless in his pursuit, in order to produce really good, interesting images with any consistency.

It boils down to the fact that you have to spend a lot of time in the woods. That, of

As a group, I really enjoy my fence-jumping photos. They are among the most difficult types of whitetail photos to produce. I've sat in fencerow blinds for hundreds of hours trying for them.

course, is not a bad thing, but to really make it work for photography, there are times when you have to be a little extreme about it. While no one can exactly plan or predict what any whitetail will do, a lot of my photography is more or less "pre-visualized." A scenario which might produce an interesting image is imagined, and the thought process goes through the basic requirements for possible success at actually getting that picture. As a photographer, I've thought my way through many such scenarios, and I'm constantly on the lookout for locations and circumstances which might have the potential to bring them to life. One good example is the sunrise photo on page 22 of this book.

During an earlier deer scouting trip to the ranch, I had noticed on two occasions that there were a couple of whitetail bucks feeding out on a wide open hill, just a little before sunrise each time. As I watched them with binoculars one morning, there was a gorgeous sunrise over the crest of the hill. I couldn't help but think what a dramatic picture it might be, if one of the bucks had been at the crest at just the right moment. Once my wheels started turning, I was determined to try for that picture. I got all of the light directions figured out exactly and set up a blind.

This particular ranch was about 80 miles from my home. Early morning photography there required that I load up and leave about 4:00 a.m., drive the 80 miles, and quickly get set up just before it would begin to get light. On these kinds of "day trips," I go to a lot of trouble to be there, even though I can never be sure what the conditions will be until I actually arrive. Early morning weather in this area can change completely in an hour, and I can't tell you how many times I've left on one of these trips in full starlight, only to have the clouds move in just before sunrise. Murphy is probably in on it.

A "panning" shot like this may test the skills of a whitetail photographer more than any other type of shot. It's a low-odds success, and a potentially high-risk waste of opportunity which could have been more certainly productive with a faster shutter speed. However, as you can see, when it works, it portrays the grace and speed of a whitetail like no other method.

At any rate, before I got "lucky" and got the photo on page 22, I made that rather arduous early morning trip for 15 mornings out of a 17 day period. I nearly got it a couple of times earlier, and several times I felt like giving up on the idea completely, but in the end I came up with almost precisely the photo I was looking for. Of course, all the times that I've tried for previsualized photos and failed, would make much less interesting stories. Nevertheless, a lot of similar efforts do eventually pay off, but rarely without a great deal of patience, persistence, and just plain old hard-headedness.

Many times, I simply have to figure out what I think it will take to get a particular type of photo. Then, if I decide that I probably won't kill myself in the process, I just try to do whatever it takes. I've slept in my blind, so I wouldn't have to disturb the area by coming in the next morning. I've driven 300 miles at a clip, to be able to photograph at specific locations for only 30 minutes. After hearing a 10 o'clock weather report one night calling for probable snow, I loaded up and left at midnight on a four-hour drive to an area where I knew I could find deer, just in case it snowed. I slept for an hour, got out in the field, and it snowed for an hour at daybreak. All traces of the snow were gone by 10 a.m., but I got my pictures. You have to be flexible in your thinking if you're going to photograph whitetail deer.

I can only imagine what some of you must be thinking by now. I'm not sure whether "insanity" should be used in

Here is another one of those shots where persistence paid off. I could never over-emphasize the importance of the simple need to be out there, time after time after time. Even though you may spend huge amounts of time waiting for something to happen, it's the only sure way to be there when the good stuff comes along. The opportunities can be as spectacular as they are brief.

defense of whitetail photographers or if it's simply a job requirement. Suffice to say that this job is not an eight-to-fiver.

After all this time in the field pursuing whitetails, it's clear that there is an incredibly diverse group of variables which will determine the nature of the photographs I'll produce. Most of the variables are well beyond my control, so I've tried to learn to work with all kinds of different situations. There are all types of weird lighting, random backgrounds, unpredictable behaviors and of course, unpredictable weather of every description. To make good whitetail photos is to make the most of whatever conditions you happen to have at the time. After some thought, I've come up with my own definition of **whitetail photography**. It would be characterized as **an endless series of repetitive attempts, to obtain impossible photographs, of unpredictable subjects, performing unlikely behaviors, at inaccessible locations, under outrageous circumstances and conditions.** Whitetails. You've just gotta love 'em.

This is one of my most famous photographs. This spectacular buck displays the regal bearing of a great whitetail buck, perhaps as grandly as any buck I've ever seen. To see and photograph him was a rare privilege. If there is any such thing as an all-American whitetail buck, this is probably the man.